The Unrepentant Church

The Unrepentant Church
*A Call to Grace, Truth, and
The Restoration of Christ's Body*

Mark E. Norton

SOULFISHER
PRESS
LLC

Copyright © 2025 Mark E. Norton
All rights reserved.

No part of this book may be reproduced, stored in a retrieval system, or transmitted in any form or by any means—electronic, mechanical, photocopying, recording, or otherwise—without the prior written permission of the publisher, except in the case of brief quotations embodied in critical articles or reviews.

Unless otherwise noted, all Scripture quotations are taken from the Holy Bible, New International Version®. Copyright © 1973, 1978, 1984, 2011 by Biblica, Inc.™ Used by permission. All rights reserved worldwide.

Scripture quotations marked "The Message" are taken from *The Message: The Bible in Contemporary Language* by Eugene H. Peterson,
© 2002 by Eugene H. Peterson. Used by permission of NavPress. All rights reserved.

Cover Art: Concept and design by Mark Norton, with assistance from ChatGPT and DALL·E (OpenAI).

This is a work of nonfiction. All real persons referenced by name have been included with respect, and any resemblance to fictionalized characters is coincidental unless otherwise stated. The views expressed in this book are solely those of the author and do not necessarily reflect those of any affiliated organizations, churches, or publishers.

Printed in the United States of America.
First edition.
ISBN: 979-8-9992520-0-5
Library of Congress Control Number: 2025912682

Soulfisher Press, LLC
Troutdale, Oregon

Dedication

This book is dedicated to Kurt, Joe, Katie, and Stefan of The Upper Room. Your ministry provided healing and opportunity for growth when I felt I no longer belonged in the church. It was your admission of imperfection, your honesty, your focus on questions rather than the answers, and your inclusion that made the Christian community real for me again. Thank you, and may God bless you in your endeavors.

Table of Contents

Preface	ix
Part I - Diagnosis	
A Church That Lost Its Way	3
Grace as the Defining Mark of Christ	9
A Culture That Devours Its Wounded	15
Rejection in the Name of Holiness	19
When the Wounded Are Blamed	24
Grace for the Guilty	31
Rejection, Not Redemption	38
Part II - The Redemptive Cure	
When the Church Repents	51
The Culture of Grace	56
From Control to Compassion	62
Discipleship That Heals	72
The Ministry of Restoration	78
Step 1: When Truth Breaks the Silence	81
Step 2: Care Before Control	84
Step 3: Listening for the Wound	87
Step 4: Healing from the Inside Out	90
Step 5: Accountability That Restores	94
Step 6: Restoration with Wisdom	97
Collateral Damage and Secondary Wounds	100

When the Fallen Refuse Help	105
The Church as a Restoring Community	108
Pastoring with Scars	110
Structures That Serve the Spirit	116
The Role of the Congregation	123
When Churches Repent	129
The Power of Lament	136
The Sound of Honest Worship	141
The Church with Open Arms	145
Signs of a Restored Church	149
Becoming the Church Jesus Died For	154
Study Guide	161

Preface

This book was born in grief. Not just my grief, but the grief of many who have been wounded by the very place meant to be a refuge—the church. It was never supposed to be this way. The body of Christ was designed for grace, for reconciliation, for mutual healing and transformation. Instead, many have experienced shame, exile, or silence when faced with the realization that they were imperfect. It has happened to people I love, it has happened to me, and since you are reading this, it may have happened to you.

This is not a book of bitterness. It is a book of burden. A burden that is borne deep in the soul. A burden to call the church back to its roots—not to defend its reputation, but to restore its soul, and to bring healing to its many victims.

However, what ultimately motivated me to write this book was a decision made by a church board that profoundly affected a family I love. The associate pastor, a man who had walked in the light of sexual addiction recovery with honesty and humility, was dismissed over social media interactions deemed inappropriate. He was a man loved by many and honest about his struggles. The board acted swiftly, terminating him without dialogue or a plan for restoration. Instead, a public statement was made, and the matter was closed. Although the interactions were unhealthy, the actions of the church leadership were more damaging than his comments ever could have been. The ripples of that decision fractured relationships, alienated his family from the church, and left many in the community questioning whether grace was merely a concept we preach—or a reality we live.

This is not a unique story. Churches across the country have struggled with how to address sin, failure, and moral lapses, particularly among their leaders. Some clamp down, others hide it. Some deflect. Few restore. However, what I saw missing in all of it was a Christlike model of grace-driven discipline. A path that allows for accountability without exile. Restoration without denial. Repentance without shame. Healing without hiding.

I do not write this as an outsider, nor as someone with all the answers. I write as someone who has felt the sting of misapplied discipline and the ache of disconnection. I write as someone who loves the church enough to tell the truth. Not to tear it down, but to build it up. Nevertheless, this is not just a leadership issue. The culture that wounded so many is sustained in part by our silence, our fears, and our failure to see each other honestly in the pews.

My hope is that this book will serve as a guide for churches, pastors, boards, and believers who are willing to walk the messy path of repentance and restoration. If we are to be the body of Christ, we must become a place where wounds are not hidden but healed. A place where leaders can be flawed and still find support. A place where love really does cover a multitude of sins.

If you have ever been wounded by a church, I hope this book makes you feel seen. If you have ever had to lead through moral failure, I hope it gives you tools. If you have ever sat on a board wondering what to do, I hope it brings clarity. Moreover, if you are still in the middle of the mess, wondering if God is still in it, I pray this helps you find hope.

We are the unrepentant church, not because we are defiant, but because we have forgotten how to repent well. Let us learn again. For the sake of Christ. For the sake of each other.

If this book speaks to something you've experienced—or long for in the Church—I'd love to hear from you: markn@soulfisher.com.

Toward a better way,
Mark E. Norton

Part I -Diagnosis

1

A Church That Lost Its Way

For many who grew up in the church, there was a time when it felt like home—a place of joy, of belonging, of truth wrapped in love. Nevertheless, over time, for too many of us, that feeling eroded. The songs remained. The messages still spoke of grace. The prayers echoed with promises of mercy. However, somewhere along the way, the way itself was lost.

We did not lose the truth. If anything, we clung to it tighter. We did not lose Scripture. We quoted it more. However, we lost the spirit in which it was meant to be lived. We became fixated on order, on standards, on image. We learned to polish the outside of the cup while quietly ignoring the cracks beneath the surface.

Jesus did not come to perfect the religious system. He came to redeem people from it. Yet we keep building systems He never endorsed, structures more concerned with behavior than belief, appearance than authenticity. We forget that His harshest words were reserved for the religious elite who strained gnats and swallowed camels, who kept people from God by the very rules they claimed honored Him.

I have seen this firsthand. I have been part of it. I have helped perpetuate it, not out of malice, but out of fear. Fear that if we let grace go too far, people might abuse it. Fear that if we tell the truth about our brokenness, we might lose our platform. Fear that if we let leaders be human, the whole thing might unravel. So we built a version of the church that hid its flaws. A version of the church that taught discipleship as conformity. Where laypeople were rewarded more for mirroring than maturing. Where sameness was mistaken for sanctification. A version of the church where sin was punished, not healed.

The result? A generation of believers who know how to act the part in public but are afraid to admit, even in church, when they are struggling. A generation of leaders who burn out or fall hard because they had no safe place to confess. A church that speaks of grace but operates in shame. Furthermore, the shame is not limited to a top-down approach only. It lives in hushed small groups, in awkward glances, in the stories we never tell because we fear they will unseat us from belonging.

This chapter is not about blame. It is about honesty. It is about recognizing that somewhere, we traded the messy beauty of real community for the sterile safety of religious performance. It is about beginning the journey back.

Because Christ did not die for a perfect church. He died for the person still sitting in the back row, wondering if this place is safe to be known. He died for a broken one. He died for us.

If we are to reclaim the heart of the gospel, we must begin here: with the humility to say we lost our way, and the courage to ask Christ to lead us home. However, even in our wandering, the world needs the Church.

Not the Church of image and authority, but the Church of Jesus—humble, honest, and healing. In a world fractured by politics, poisoned by outrage, and numbed by apathy, the Church remains God's chosen vessel to bring reconciliation, however, only if we are willing to reconcile ourselves.

This is not the time for retreat. It is the time for repentance—not just from individual sin, but from institutional pride, and from the quiet complicity of the crowd that lets the institution drift unchecked. From pretending to have all the answers instead of listening to the pain. From wielding truth as a weapon rather than a balm.

The Church is not obsolete. It is essential. However, only if it returns to its essence: people transformed by grace, bound together in love, living with authenticity, and extending the same mercy they have received.

The story of the church is not yet finished. It is still being written—in every community, in every heart willing to say, "We missed it, but we want to find it again." That search does not begin with strategies or sermons. It begins with humility. With the courage to admit that sometimes, the institution called to proclaim the good news has instead inflicted pain.

Our refusal to deal honestly with our imperfections has cost us dearly. The watching world sees our polished surfaces and wonders what lies beneath. They hear our claims of love but encounter judgment. They see power more than compassion. The church must learn to weep again—for its failures, for its pride, for those it has pushed away.

True repentance is not a PR campaign. It is not about managing optics. It is about sitting in the dust and ashes, like Job, and meeting God anew. It is about listening to the wounded and resisting the urge to defend ourselves. It is about remembering that the church is not the savior. Christ is. Moreover, He still walks among the broken, offering healing—not for show, but because He loves.

There is still hope. The prodigal can come home. The elder brother can join the celebration. The Pharisee can trade status for surrender. However, it starts with us. With us letting go of the need to appear right and embracing the call to be made right.

Before we move forward, we must go deeper. Into humility. Into confession. Into Christ.

When Jesus cleansed the temple, it was not because worship had ceased—it was because worship had become corrupted. The marketplace had invaded the holy place. In our time, the intrusion is more subtle. We have traded the cross for fancy logos, repentance for rebranding, and holiness for stagecraft. It is still worship, but it is not worthy.

We see declining church attendance and think the answer is better marketing, more polished sermons, or flashier services. What people long for is not spectacle—it is substance. They want to know if God truly changes lives, if grace actually heals wounds, and if the church is more than a club for the already convinced.

The hunger is real, and the world is watching. What they see too often is a church scrambling to preserve itself rather than pouring itself out. They see leadership structures more concerned with control than care, prioritizing image over integrity. However, structure alone does not wound—it is the silence of the many that often allows harm to linger. When scandals arise, as they inevitably do, they see a cover-up instead of a confession.

We must do better, not for survival's sake, but for the gospel's sake.

This book begins with pain because healing never happens without it. This book begins with confession because revival never begins without repentance. Furthermore, this book begins with loss—of trust, of innocence, of clarity—because that is often where God begins something new.

So let the reckoning come, not as condemnation, but as invitation. Let us dare to believe that the Church can still be what Christ intended. Let us repent of every time we chose silence over solidarity, performance over presence, exclusion over embrace.

Let us remember that the Church was birthed not in a boardroom or a branding meeting, but in an upper room—with fear, with trembling, with prayer. The Holy Spirit did not descend upon a stage with a spotlight but upon a circle of scared and hopeful believers, huddled together in longing. The Spirit came not for the polished, the pedigreed, or the powerful, but for the hungry, the humble, and the honest. It came upon a room full of imperfect men and women, chosen not for their qualifications but for their hunger for more and their willingness to be used.

Let us return there, not in location, but in posture. Let us seek again the heart of a church birthed in dependence, not dominance; in surrender, not spectacle.

Let us also acknowledge the subtle idolatry that creeps into church culture. The idol of success. The idol of celebrity. The idol of safety. We build kingdoms in His name but forget to make Him King. We measure effectiveness by attendance and giving, not by humility or justice. In the pursuit of relevance, we risk losing reverence.

The call to repentance is not a call to despair but to freedom. It is an invitation to drop the heavy cloak of religious performance and step into the light of God's presence. It is the first step toward becoming a community where people can breathe again, where masks fall off, and where love covers a multitude of sins.

The church must once again become a hospital, not a courtroom. A place where wounds are treated, not displayed. Where accountability does not mean punishment, but support. Where leaders are allowed to heal. Where the gospel is not a slogan, but a lifeline. Where every member, not just pastors, becomes a keeper of grace. Where people do not have to audition to be accepted, where the tired and bruised can say, 'I am not okay,' and be met with compassion, not correction.

We cannot change the past, but we can confront it. We can confess our complicity in cultures of silence, of shame, of control. Furthermore, in doing so, we make space for something better.

Something holy. Something true.

If we are brave enough to grieve, God will be faithful to rebuild. If we are humble enough to listen, the Spirit will be faithful to lead. If we are honest enough to admit that we have been wrong, Christ will be faithful to make us right.

This is not just a call to the church as an institution. It is a call to each of us. To every elder who has looked the other way. To every pastor who has carried burdens in silence. To every believer who has felt they could not speak up. This is our moment to say, "No more."

No more hiding. No more fear. No more pretending. Let us repent. Let us rise.

The words of the prophet Isaiah serve as a prophetic message to us today, just as they did when first delivered:

> *"Quit your worship charades. I cannot stand your trivial religious games: Monthly conferences, weekly Sabbaths, special meetings—meetings, meetings, meetings—I cannot stand one more! Meetings for this, meetings for that. I hate them! You've worn me out! I'm sick of your religion, religion, religion, while you go right on sinning. When you put on your next prayer-performance, I'll be looking the other way. No matter how long or loud or often you pray, I'll not be listening. And do you know why? Because you've been tearing people to pieces, and your hands are bloody. Go home and wash up. Clean up your act. Sweep your lives clean of your evil doings so I do not have to look at them any longer. Say no to wrong.*
>
> *Learn to do good. Work for justice. Help the down-and-out. Stand up for the homeless. Go to bat for the defenseless."* —Isaiah 1:13-17 (The Message)

2
Grace as the Defining Mark of Christ

When Jesus walked the earth, He spent time with outcasts, dined with sinners, touched lepers, defended adulterers, and dignified the overlooked. He did not flinch at the scandal of association. He leaned into it. Not because He endorsed sin, but because He loved sinners. He knew that love is the soil in which transformation takes root.

If we count ourselves as believers, we must remember that we too were once outsiders—estranged from God, shaped by brokenness, and burdened by sin. We were not invited into His presence because we had cleaned ourselves up; we were met by grace in the midst of our ruin. That is the place where He found us, not at our best, but at our worst. If He could extend such mercy to us in that condition, how can we withhold it from others?

Grace does not mean ignoring sin. It means refusing to define people by it. It means seeing the image of God where others see only shame. It means recognizing that healing begins with belonging. Before Jesus ever said, "Go and sin no more," He offered protection, honor, and peace.

Consider the woman caught in adultery. Dragged into public shame, used as a pawn in a theological trap, her fate seemed sealed. Unexpectedly, Jesus knelt beside her. He did not deny the law. He simply exposed its misuse. "Let the one without sin cast the first stone." One by one, the accusers left. Jesus, the only sinless one, was in a position to condemn her. However, He did not. He extended grace. He gave her the dignity of standing. Then He spoke the truth. Grace first. Truth second. And always in that order.

This is not weakness. This is power restrained by love.

We see this pattern again and again. With Zacchaeus, a despised tax collector, Jesus did not demand repentance before offering fellowship. He invited Himself to dinner. The invitation itself ignited transformation. Zacchaeus stood up and gave half his possessions to the poor. Grace made space for repentance.

One by one, we could go through the apostles and examine their faults—their impulsiveness, doubts, jealousy, pride, and fear—but Christ called them as they were.

Peter denied Him. Thomas doubted Him. James and John jockeyed for position. Judas betrayed Him. Yet, Christ extended the call anyway. He did not choose them for their perfection; He chose them for their willingness to follow Him. He saw in them not just who they were, but who they could become. In His presence, their flaws did not disqualify them—they became the soil in which grace could grow.

Even in Christ's final moments on the cross, grace flowed. To the thief beside Him—guilty, dying, with nothing left to offer—Jesus said, "Today, you will be with me in paradise."

And then came the words that echo through eternity, offered to those who crucified Him, and to us:

"Father, forgive them, for they know not what they do."

That is the heart of grace. Not just forgiving the repentant, but initiating forgiveness—even when repentance has not come. Grace starts the conversation. It opens the door.

However, somehow, we have managed to reverse this. We have made grace conditional. We have demanded that people clean up before we let them in. We have sent the message—intended or not—that the Church is a place for the already-fixed, not the deeply broken.

Grace as the Defining Mark of Christ

This contradiction wounds. Moreover, this contradiction is not just institutional—it is personal. It shows up in hallway glances, unspoken pain, and the smiles we fake to maintain our sense of belonging. It wounds the people trying to come home, and it wounds the credibility of our message. A gospel of grace cannot be lived out by a church of judgment; yet, we still do it.

Why? Because grace costs. It costs our sense of superiority. It costs us our need to be right. It costs us our comfort. If we are not willing to pay that price, we cannot claim to follow the one who paid everything.

There is a reason grace is hard. It levels us. It exposes the myth that some of us have earned our place. It reminds us that none of us did. The addict and the elder, the gossip and the worship leader—all of us are here by mercy.

Therefore, if we are here by mercy, then our posture must be merciful.

This is where the Church must do soul-searching. Have we made grace a slogan or a culture? Is it on our signs but absent in our boardrooms? Do our processes reflect the heart of Jesus or the fear of man? Do we offer grace when it is messy? When it is inconvenient? When it might raise eyebrows?

Too often, grace is celebrated in testimony but withheld in real time. We love the story of the prodigal when it is told in the past tense, but what about when he is still in the pigsty? When he walks through our church doors—broken, confused, reeking of his fall—do we run to him with open arms, or cross them in suspicion? When he does not yet have the words for repentance, do we speak mercy over him anyway? Or do we build a checklist for his return, hoping to see humility only if it looks like shame? Grace meets the prodigal at the threshold, not after a probation period. That is what makes it grace.

In our desire to protect the Church, have we forgotten that its founder was not concerned with self-protection? Jesus let His reputation be torn apart. He touched the unclean, honored the disgraced, and welcomed the rejected. He did not measure worthiness. He extended worth.

It is worth pausing here to reflect on what shaped the Church's defensiveness. Part of it comes from public failures. The scandals of high-profile pastors—from Jim Bakker and Jimmy Swaggart in the 1980s to more recent celebrity pastors such as Mark Driscoll, Carl Lentz, and Brian Houston—left a stain that many church leaders still try to scrub away. The response was image control: polished pulpits, spotless reputations, and a culture of secrecy. The goal was to avoid another fall. However, the strategy backfired.

In trying to project perfection, we became less honest. In trying to prevent a scandal, we lost our souls. We made church leadership more about posture than presence. We trained pastors to hide their struggles rather than share them. We, the congregation, often preferred it that way. We nodded at vulnerability but rewarded perfection. We created a culture where authenticity felt risky, not just for leaders, but for all of us.

One textbook I read during ministry training stated that pastors should never admit to personal faults, must be well-dressed, and not overweight. Think about that. Instead of calling shepherds to humility, we trained them to maintain appearances. As congregants, we often rewarded them for it, mistaking polish for anointing. No wonder so many burn out. No wonder so few feel safe. We need to realize that there is a hunger in our world for something different. Something real.

That is why I find unexpected inspiration in Jelly Roll's songs. The songs reflect a person struggling with the choices of their past as they face their faith. However, isn't that precisely for whom grace is for? Not the almost-healed, but the barely-holding-on. His music captures something the Church often misses: that brokenness does not disqualify someone from grace—it is the doorway to it. It is his raw authenticity that resonates—no performance, no pretension, just the echo of a soul desperate for mercy. That kind of honesty is what grace was made for. Imagine a church like that—a place where people can tell the truth, be met with love, and still be called higher. Not a church of compromise, but a church of compassion.

Because discipleship is not behavior modification, it is becoming more like Christ. Christ was not ashamed to stand with sinners. In fact, He was accused of being one.

Grace does not mean there are no standards. It means we walk with people as they grow into them. It means we see potential where others see problems. It means we never stop believing that redemption is possible.

The church should be the safest place to fail—and to heal.

What if our churches were more like hospitals and less like courts? What if discipline was rooted in restoration, not retribution? What if we believed that God's kindness really does lead to repentance?

Grace changes everything. It changed Zacchaeus. It changed the woman at the well. It changed me. It can change us all, but only if we let it.

Let us be a church marked not by who we keep out, but by who we bring in. Not by our perfection, but by our mercy. Not by our stance, but by our embrace.

Let us be known—not just for preaching grace, but for living it.

Let us be willing to have our hearts broken again. To cry with the hurting. To bear burdens we do not fully understand. To walk slowly with the wounded, without trying to fix them first.

Let us train leaders who lead with a limp and tenderness, not polish and distance. Let us surround our pastors with prayer, accountability, and room to be human. Let us do the same for each other. Let every pew become a place of grace, where believers carry burdens together instead of covering them up alone.

Let us reshape our communities to cherish honesty over performance, healing over hiding, process over perfection. Let grace begin with us—in the lobby, in the awkward silence after someone confesses, in the patience we offer when someone stumbles again.

Grace is not soft. It is fierce. It stares sin in the face and says, "You do not get the last word." Grace does not flinch at the mess. It runs toward it. Grace is the lifeblood of the gospel, the very thing that keeps the Church alive. If we lose grace, we lose everything. If we reclaim grace, boldly, wholly, unapologetically, we might just find our way again.

Then maybe the world will see Christ in us, not as a theory or a doctrine, but as a living, breathing reality. The One who touched lepers. The One who dined with sinners. The One who still whispers to the guilty, "Go in peace."

3
A Culture That Devours Its Wounded

> *"The greatest harm done to the wounded is not their fall, but our refusal to kneel beside them."*
> — *Unknown*

If grace is meant to be the heartbeat of the Church, then how have we become a place that often expels rather than embraces the broken? The Church is called to be a refuge, a hospital for the hurting, a family for the fallen. However, in too many cases, it becomes a tribunal—a place where sin is spotlighted, shame is weaponized, and restoration is replaced by rejection. We have built systems that protect appearances but damage souls. We have exchanged shepherding for management, and in doing so, we have failed the very ones Christ came to save.

Some of the deepest wounds people carry are not from the world, but from the Church. These wounds come not only from personal failures but from how spiritual authorities handled those failures. There are countless stories of people who, having confessed a struggle or a sin, found themselves shunned, discredited, or quietly pushed to the margins. Not walked with. Not discipled. Not restored. Just removed.

In an effort to maintain moral purity or protect the institution, we have often sacrificed the individual. We act as if grace must be guarded, lest someone take advantage of it. However, grace, by definition, is unguarded. It is undeserved. The moment we put a price on it, it ceases to be grace.

Consider the Apostle Peter. After denying Christ three times in Jesus' darkest hour, Peter returned to fishing. He had failed spectacularly. Jesus did not send someone to replace him. He went to him. He made breakfast for him. He asked him three times, "Do you love me?"—not to shame him, but to restore him. Each affirmation reversed a denial. Grace was extended. Purpose was re-commissioned. Then Peter went on to lead the early Church.

Now, compare that to how many churches deal with moral failure today. A pastor stumbles, and instead of surrounding him with care and accountability, we exile him. Too often, we, the congregation, stay silent or complicit, uncomfortable with brokenness that mirrors our own. However, silence in the face of failure is not safety—it is surrender. We fear scandal more than we love the fallen. We treat failure as final. Nevertheless, Jesus never did.

We also see this contrast in Paul's shifting view of John Mark. In Acts 15, Paul refuses to take Mark on a missionary journey because he had previously abandoned the work. However, later on, Paul writes from prison and says, "Get Mark and bring him with you, because he is helpful to me in my ministry." 2 Timothy 4:11 (NIV) Somewhere along the way, restoration happened. Trust was rebuilt. Mark was not discarded forever. He was welcomed back.

What happens when a church does not allow that process? When an individual is cast out before grace can do its work? We lose not only that person, but also the testimony of what God might have done through them. We create orphans when we are called to create disciples.

A Culture That Devours Its Wounded

Some argue that harsh consequences are necessary to uphold the Church's witness. That letting sinners remain among us will damage our credibility. What greater witness is there than a community that mirrors the heart of Christ—a heart that heals, restores, and reclaims? The watching world already knows we sin. What they need to see is how we love.

Yes, sin must be addressed. Yes, accountability matters. Discipline in the Kingdom is not about punishment—it is about restoration. Its goal is not to push people out, but to bring them back in. The model is always redemptive. Always relational. Always shaped by grace.

Restorative discipline creates space for confession, establishes boundaries for healing, and invites community support, not exile. It balances truth with tenderness, accountability with affirmation.

When we devour our wounded, we betray our mission. We trade grace for gatekeeping. We lose compassion in our critique. We become institutions more interested in preserving policies than in restoring people.

Imagine a church where confession is not met with scandal, but with support, where the response to sin is not isolation, but intentional relationship, where leaders lead from humility, not hierarchy. Where people can walk in with their wounds visible, and be loved toward healing instead of judged toward hiding.

We were never meant to be a courtroom. We were meant to be a home.

Jesus told the story of the Good Shepherd who leaves the ninety-nine to find the one. Not to scold it. Not to lecture it. Instead, he carries it home on His shoulders. That is the gospel. That is our model. If that is not how we are functioning, then something has gone terribly wrong.

In the early Church, unity and mercy were not just ideals; they were necessities. Acts 2 describes a community marked by shared meals, shared burdens, and daily growth. It was a messy, generous, grace-filled movement that drew people in. We must recover that ethos.

We must resist the temptation to distance ourselves from the fallen just to protect our image. Jesus did not manage perceptions—He embodied grace, even when it cost Him His reputation. He was mocked, misunderstood, and maligned because of the people He chose to love. If we want to follow Him, we must be willing to bear the same cost.

Because when the Church devours its wounded, it devours its own credibility. Its own compassion. Its own calling. However, when we restore the wounded, we become what we were always meant to be: the hands and feet of a Savior who still walks toward sinners, still calls the broken, and still believes in redemption. We reflect the face of Christ—scarred, risen, and still reaching.

4
Rejection in the Name of Holiness

> *"It is not the healthy who need a doctor, but the sick. I have not come to call the righteous, but sinners to repentance."*
> — Jesus (Luke 5:31–32)

We have come to believe that protecting the Church means purging the impure. That spiritual health is best preserved through insulation rather than transformation. The outcome is a system where fear dictates behavior—where those who sin are treated not as patients in need of care, but as pathogens to be removed. Tragically, this approach disguises itself as biblical fidelity when, in truth, it is spiritual malpractice.

This is not the holiness Jesus modeled.

A Pharisaical Return

The Pharisees of Jesus' time were deeply committed to holiness. They memorized scripture, attended every gathering, fasted, tithed, and prayed aloud in public. However, they also imposed burdens on others and distanced themselves from the very people Jesus spent time with. They worshiped a God of mercy with lips that delivered judgment.

"Woe to you Pharisees, because you give God a tenth of your mint, rue, and all other kinds of garden herbs, but you neglect justice and the love of God. You should have practiced the latter without leaving the former undone." Luke 11:42 (NIV)

When Jesus touched the leper, ate with tax collectors, and defended the adulterous woman, He was not rejecting holiness—He was revealing its truest form. He was demonstrating with His life that holiness is not a retreat from the mess of humanity, but a compassionate, redemptive presence within it.

Holiness, in its essence, is not about withdrawal. It is about presence. It is about being set apart for others, not from them. It is about becoming vessels of light in dark places, not fortresses against the darkness. It is incarnational. It goes where the need is deepest.

However, many churches have become fortresses. Afraid of being seen as soft on sin, they grow hard on sinners. In doing so, they inadvertently make grace conditional and belonging transactional. Holiness becomes a weapon, not a witness.

The Culture of Cleanliness

There is an unspoken rule in many congregations: if you have problems, be discreet. If you struggle, do it silently. If you confess, be prepared for consequences. These rules are not written in church bylaws, but they are deeply felt.

Young couples who confess sexual sin before marriage are denied wedding ceremonies. Divorced individuals are disqualified from leadership roles. Men and women battling addiction are told to get clean before joining small groups. Pastors are pressured to hide their mental health struggles for fear of losing credibility.

These are not hypotheticals; they are the stories of real people. The Church, meant to be a place of healing, becomes a place of hiding. The cost of authenticity is exile.

The message becomes clear: acceptance depends on appearance. Belonging hinges on behaving. That is not the gospel. The gospel begins with God loving us in our worst, not rewarding us at our best.

When Jesus encountered sinners, He did not give them a checklist. He gave them Himself. Transformation followed acceptance. The Church today often reverses that order.

Jesus and the Bleeding Woman

A significant moment in Jesus' ministry was His interaction with the woman who had been bleeding for twelve years. She was unclean by every religious standard. The temple rejected her. She was likely destitute, desperate, and alone.

However, when she reached for Jesus, He did not recoil. He did not chastise her for touching Him in her state. He stopped. He saw her. He called her "Daughter." Furthermore, He declared her clean.

He healed her not just physically but socially. He gave her back her name. He restored her dignity. Moreover, in doing so, He modeled the heart of God toward the rejected.

Jesus did not fear contamination. He embodied restoration.

This should be the model for our churches. Too often, instead of welcoming the bleeding, we demand they heal first. We expect people to present themselves as whole before we will call them family. It is grace after graduation—completely backward.

When Rejection Is Mistaken for Righteousness

In our efforts to uphold righteousness, we sometimes drift into self-righteousness. We confuse moral vigilance with spiritual maturity. We protect the institution rather than reflect the Savior. We become more concerned with the reputation of the Church than the redemption of the individual.

We forget that Jesus warned more harshly against religious pride than He did against sexual immorality. He flipped tables in the temple, not at the city gate. His harshest rebukes were aimed not at the prostitutes, but at the proud.

When a church removes a leader because they sinned, but offers no pathway to restoration, it is not practicing holiness. It is practicing image management. When a congregation gossips about a fallen member but never prays for them, it is not walking in truth. It is walking in judgment.

Jesus had every right to judge, and yet He chose mercy. That is what made Him so scandalous, and yet so divine.

Holiness That Heals

True holiness is attractive. It draws people toward God. It is rooted in humility and fueled by love. Holiness without love is cruelty. Righteousness without embodying grace is tyranny.

Discipline without restoration is just punishment, plain and simple.

The Church is called to uphold moral standards, yes, but more than that, it is called to embody Christ. That means we lead with compassion. We restore with gentleness. We confront with tears, not triumph.

We must ask ourselves: Do our policies reflect the heart of Jesus or the fears of man? Are we guarding truth or guarding comfort? Are we protecting the Church from sin, or preventing the sinner from healing?

If the Church cannot be the place where people are safe to fall and still find love, then it will cease to be the Church at all.

Holiness in Practice: What It Looks Like

Holiness in practice means confronting sin honestly, but without condemnation. It means saying hard things in love. It means creating an environment where confession is not the end of the road, but the beginning of a healing process. We do not celebrate the sin, but we should welcome the willing confession.

Imagine a church where accountability includes grace, where every act of confrontation is paired with a plan of care.

Rejection in the Name of Holiness

Where leaders meet regularly not to monitor behavior but to mentor character.

It also means recognizing that holiness is not uniformity. People grow at different paces. Some struggle in areas we do not understand. Holiness is not about having it all together; it is about yielding daily to the God who holds us together.

It requires courage. Because healing is messy. Grace is risky. Nevertheless, Jesus risked everything to redeem us. He left heaven's perfection for earth's imperfection. If we are to follow Him, we must walk the same path.

A Call to Return

It is time to return to the holiness of Jesus. A holiness that kneels in the dirt. That touches the untouchable. That walks toward the tomb, not away from it. That weeps at brokenness but never turns its face.

We do not become holy by isolating ourselves from the world. We become holy by being transformed in the presence of God, by God, and then carrying that presence to others. Our holiness should never be a wall; it should be a window. A window through which the world sees Jesus.

Rejection is easy. Restoration is costly. It is the cost Jesus bore, and if we claim His name, we must bear it too.

May we pray, "Let us stop rejecting in the name of holiness. Let us start restoring in the name of Christ. Let us be a Church that embraces the messy, the wounded, the prodigal, the doubting, and the undone. Let us love like Jesus. Let us be holy, not by how far we stand from the broken, but by how closely we walk with them." Then let us be the answer to that prayer.

5
When the Wounded Are Blamed

> *"They dress the wound of my people as though it were not serious. 'Peace, peace,' they say, when there is no peace."* — Jeremiah 6:14 (NIV)

In the aftermath of failure, pain, or crisis within the church, blame often becomes the default posture. Instead of offering support, the community may seek someone to hold accountable, not out of a sense of justice, but out of discomfort. Churches often feel more at ease addressing a scapegoat than entering into the uncomfortable process of sitting with brokenness.

This tendency is not new. From the Garden of Eden, where Adam blamed Eve and Eve blamed the serpent, humanity has leaned into blame rather than healing. But in Christ's Church, the pattern should be different. Unfortunately, too often, it is not.

When the Wounded are Blamed

Victim or Villain?

It is not always the transgressor that the church seeks to isolate itself from. In many modern church scenarios, the line between victim and villain is blurred by assumptions, gossip, and image management. When a member of a congregation is hurt by another, especially by someone in leadership, the church's response often prioritizes damage control over justice and care.

Victims are sometimes asked, or pressured, if honest, to forgive too quickly, often without the support they need to process the trauma. If they resist, they may be labeled bitter, unforgiving, or divisive. This framing puts the burden on the wounded to maintain unity, even when their wounds are fresh and bleeding.

Take, for example, cases of spiritual abuse. A pastor oversteps boundaries, manipulates scripture, or uses their authority to control others. When someone speaks up, the focus is frequently not on the abuse but on how the accuser might be harming the church's reputation. Instead of becoming advocates for the wounded, some churches circle the wagons to protect the leader.

I have seen this firsthand in my time of service in a church. The lead pastor told me that whenever someone left this church, he was confident that they had been reading the book "The Subtle Power of Spiritual Abuse" by David Johnson. He detested the book, although I do not know that he actually read it. Later, I, too, left that church—the church where I had served on staff as an associate pastor. I was removed from this volunteer position on a Sunday morning, after I questioned the pastor's motives for scheduling staff meetings when I could not attend, despite having just told me I was an important part of the church. He immediately announced it to the congregation that morning. For clarification, I had not, and still have not, read that book, but I feel I have lived it.

It is a tragic pattern: silence the hurting to protect the powerful. However, Jesus consistently did the opposite. He stopped for the woman who bled. He shielded the woman caught in adultery. He noticed the one cast out of the synagogue. He dignified the abused and challenged the abusers.

The Idol of Image

Much of this blame-shifting behavior is rooted in the idolization of reputation. Churches, especially large ones, may feel that they have much to lose—donors, attendance, and influence—if a scandal takes root. Leaders become symbols of spiritual success, and any blemish is seen as a threat. So, when a problem arises, the question is not always, "How can we best reflect Christ?" but "How can we best preserve our image?"

The answer often involves minimizing the issue, silencing the victim, or redirecting the narrative. In those moments, the church trades compassion for control, managing optics instead of ministering grace.

The gospel was never meant to be managed; it was meant to be lived. Jesus embraced scandal to reach the broken. He ate with sinners, welcomed the unclean, and endured the shame of the cross.

Costly Compassion

Real compassion is never convenient. It is costly. It takes time, emotional energy, and spiritual maturity. It refuses to let a hurting person walk alone. It resists the temptation to explain away pain. It does not ask the wounded to hurry up and heal for the sake of comfort.

Churches that embody this kind of compassion are rare, but they do exist. They are the communities that sit in silence with the grieving, offer therapy and spiritual guidance, and refuse to sacrifice people for reputation. They believe the Church should be the safest place for the wounded to come, because they understand that their Savior still bears scars.

I have experienced such a church. After leaving the church where I had served, I came to a community known as The Upper Room in Minneapolis. It was an incredible community that evolved into a church, serving as a place of healing for many, including me. Never had I experienced a church where the pastor was as transparent about his own faults and challenges, nor a church as focused on making a difference in people's lives, regardless of their circumstances. This attitude was prevalent throughout the church's culture and continued long after the end of his tenure as pastor.

Gender and Blame in the Church

An especially insidious pattern emerges when women are the ones who have been harmed. Throughout church history, women have often been blamed for the moral failings of men. From Eve in the garden to Bathsheba on the rooftop, the narrative has too frequently cast women as the source of temptation rather than as individuals made in the image of God.

In churches today, this pattern can still be seen when women come forward about inappropriate behavior by male leaders or fellow congregants. Rather than receiving support, women are often met with skepticism. Questions swirl not around the behavior of the accused, but the intentions and reputations of the women who speak out. Was she trying to seduce him? Did she misunderstand? Was she seeking attention?

This behavior is not only degrading—it is damaging. It perpetuates a culture where women are less likely to report misconduct, fearing they will be judged more harshly than the offender. In this environment, silence becomes the safest option, and injustice thrives in the quiet.

Moreover, the repercussions for women who do speak up often go beyond social shunning. They may be removed from leadership, lose community, or be labeled as rebellious or disruptive to the body. Moreover, while the man may receive a slap on the wrist or a brief leave of absence, the woman's life may be irrevocably changed.

This double standard is not only poor theology—it is antithetical to the character of Christ. Jesus never blamed the wounded. He dignified them. When the woman with perfume broke it over His feet, the room judged. Jesus honored her. When the Samaritan woman spoke to Him at the well, He did not focus on her failures—He revealed her identity and His grace.

Let us not forget Mary Magdalene, who was delivered from demonic oppression and became a close follower of Jesus, one of the few at the crucifixion, and the first to witness the resurrection. Jesus entrusted a woman with the news of His victory over death. That alone should cause the Church to reconsider any theology that marginalizes or blames women.

Churches must follow His lead. They must create environments where women are safe to speak, safe to heal, and safe to serve without suspicion. Where accountability is applied equally and justice is not influenced by gender.

If the Church is to reflect Christ, it must honor all His daughters with the same reverence He did.

When Silence Speaks Volumes

There are also situations where the church's silence becomes its loudest statement. When a member is harmed—whether emotionally, physically, or spiritually—and the leadership fails to acknowledge it publicly, the message is clear: "This pain is not our concern."

Silence in the face of wrongdoing often signals complicity. A church that cannot name harm cannot heal it. Apologies are not admissions of weakness; they are the beginnings of restoration. Public wrongdoing often demands public lament.

This does not mean churches should turn confession into a spectacle, but it does mean that transparency must prevail over secrecy. Healing cannot happen in the dark.

A Theology of Suffering

Many churches are uncomfortable with suffering. In traditions that emphasize victory, healing, and breakthrough, suffering can be perceived as a theological failure. This discomfort with pain often causes churches to bypass grief and move quickly to triumph.

Scripture does not sideline suffering—it centers it. Job's story is not about quick recovery; it is about long lament. David's psalms are not all praise; many are cries of desperation. Jesus wept. Jesus sweated blood. Jesus died.

The Church needs to reclaim a theology that allows space for woundedness. Not every pain has a quick fix. Not every story wraps up neatly. And not every person in pain will be able to move on within a timeframe that others deem appropriate.

Sometimes, the most spiritual thing a church can do is say, "We do not know why this happened, but we will walk with you through it."

Rebuilding Trust

For those who have been blamed when they were the ones bleeding, returning to church can be difficult. Trust has been broken. Words like "grace" and "community" may feel hollow.

Churches must recognize this and do the hard work of rebuilding trust, not demanding it. This begins with listening—truly listening. Not for the sake of response or defense, but for understanding. It requires leadership to be vulnerable and open to learning. It demands a shift from power to service.

Rebuilding trust takes time. And the effort must be consistent. One healing sermon or one kind letter will not erase the memory of blame. But humility and consistency can start to create a new witness.

A Better Witness

When the world looks at the Church, it should not see a courtroom of judges. It should be a hospital of healers. A family of the forgiven. A community that names sin, yes—but never weaponizes it.

The Church must remember that Jesus died not just for sinners, but as one in the eyes of the world. He bore the blame He did not deserve, so that we could stand uncondemned. If we truly believe that, we must stop blaming the wounded. We must start binding up their wounds.

6
Grace for the Guilty

In the previous chapter, we examined how a culture of grace transforms the way we live and love. Now we must ask: What does that culture look like when guilt is real and fresh?

At the heart of the gospel is this unshakable truth: grace is for the guilty.

Nevertheless, within the modern Church, this truth has too often been obscured by the need to manage appearances. Instead of being a place where the fallen are restored, the Church has sometimes become a place where guilt is punished and grace withheld—unless, of course, the guilty are powerful or well-connected.

The Scandal of Grace

Grace, when rightly understood, is always scandalous. It defies logic. It is unearned, undeserved, and often seems unfair. To the wounded, grace may feel like betrayal. To the self-righteous, it may feel like a compromise. However, to the sinner who knows their need, it feels like life.

Nothing in my life demonstrates this truth more than experiences with a fellow brother. This brother loved to witness on the street, embracing the style of Ray Comfort with the pointed questions of "Have you ever told a lie? Have you ever stolen anything? Have you ever lusted after someone of the opposite sex? If so, then you have just admitted you are a lying, thieving, adulterer and are going to hell." Surely not the message of let him who is without sin cast the first stone. This brother completed his pastoral training, came on staff at the church, and then soon admitted to having an ongoing affair. Grace was never a topic on his lips.

Everything was black and white, no room for grace. Had he understood grace, and had we built a culture that practiced it together, those of us around him may have been able to help him through repentance, healing, and reconciliation.

Grace is the very heart of the gospel. From the moment Jesus extended forgiveness to the woman caught in adultery, to the thief on the cross, to Peter after denial, He demonstrated that guilt was never the end of the story for those who turn back to Him.

We need to recapture that vision of grace, not as a free pass or a soft word for sin, but as a radical force of redemption. Grace never denies guilt. It acknowledges it fully and still offers restoration.

Grace in the Dirt

One of the most compelling stories in the New Testament is found in John 8. A woman caught in the very act of adultery is thrown before Jesus. Her accusers are ready to stone her. The law is clear. She is guilty.

Jesus says nothing at first. He bends down and writes in the dirt. When He does speak, His words are piercing: "Let any one of you who is without sin be the first to throw a stone at her."

Silence. One by one, the accusers drop their stones and walk away.

Jesus stands, looks the woman in the eye, and says, "Has no one condemned you?" "No one, sir," she replies.

"Then neither do I condemn you," Jesus declares. "Go now and leave your life of sin."

He does not excuse her sin. He does not minimize it. Rather, He refuses to let it define her future.

He sees beyond her guilt to her possibility. That is grace in action.

If Jesus stooped down and got dirty for the guilty, how can His Church stay standing on the sidelines?

Picture a man who has fallen into a muddy ditch. Some churches stand at the edge and yell instructions on how to climb out. Others walk by, unwilling to be stained. However, a church shaped by grace jumps in, lifts the man, and walks with him—even if it means getting dirty.

Imagine that it is not just one person reaching down, but many. A church of rescuers, arms outstretched, working together. That is the Church Jesus envisioned. That is the Church the world is dying to see.

Too often, instead of reaching down, the Church backs away. When we do engage, our models often reflect fear and control more than the grace we claim to embody.

The Failure of Modern Disciplinary Models

Many churches claim to have a process for dealing with sin, but often that process is punitive and opaque—redemption in name only. A moral failure, a poor decision, or even an ill-advised comment can result in a swift and quiet removal. There is no path to restoration offered, only silence and exclusion.

I have seen this firsthand. I have watched leaders fall and be immediately exiled—without any process, conversation, or opportunity for growth. Sometimes these decisions are made out of fear. Other times, they are made to "protect the flock," as if the mere presence of a broken person threatens the purity of the whole.

Christ never modeled exile for the broken—He modeled presence. He walked alongside them, touched their wounds, and called them back to life. His harshest rebukes were not aimed at the sinners He healed, but at the religious elite who withheld compassion and grace. This posture of mercy reveals the very heart of the gospel: restoration over rejection, healing over humiliation.

Judas, though later known for his betrayal, was caught stealing from the disciples' collective funds—yet Jesus did not remove him from the group. He continued to walk with Judas, allowing room for change. That does not excuse what came later, but it reminds us: even repeated failure did not result in immediate exile. Jesus modeled patient presence, not preemptive dismissal.

It is essential to distinguish between accountability and exile. Accountability involves relationship, instruction, and a path forward; exile brings rejection, shame, and abandonment.

Grace Is Not the Opposite of Holiness

There is a concern in some church circles that the concept of grace leads to permissiveness. That if we emphasize forgiveness too much, people will sin more. We must be reminded that it is not what Scripture teaches. Paul anticipated this concern in Romans 6: "Shall we go on sinning so that grace may increase? By no means!"

Grace does not ignore sin—it changes the heart. It empowers people to live differently. The one who has been forgiven much loves much. Grace does not weaken holiness; it fuels it. When we know we are loved even at our worst, we are more likely to become our best.

Churches that emphasize grace create cultures of transformation, not indulgence. They model the patience of God. They invest in people. They give second chances, and third, and fourth.

Grace and Leadership

Perhaps the most difficult place to extend grace is toward leaders who fall. Pastors, elders, deacons—when they fail, the ripple effects are immense. The pain can be deep, the betrayal real.

Understand that these are still human beings, loved by God. Their calling does not exempt them from struggle. Their position does not make them immune to temptation. If anything, the pressures they face may increase the likelihood of the fall.

This does not mean leaders should escape accountability, far from it. However, accountability should never mean abandonment. A leader who confesses, repents, and seeks healing should be given a path toward restoration, not to their title necessarily, but to their place in the community and their identity in Christ.

I have served on boards where we had to confront the moral failure of leaders. Sadly, I must confess that the response was often cold and reactionary. I wish I could say that grace was the guiding principle, but I, too, have had my failures that I wrestle with and need to cover with grace. Its application starts with us.

Moreover, it does not end with us. Every member of the Church must wrestle with the challenge and beauty of grace, because failure is not exclusive to leaders. We all need paths to healing, hope, and restoration.

Grace Is the Culture of the Cross

The cross was the greatest act of justice and the greatest act of grace in one moment. Jesus took on the punishment for our guilt so we could receive the reward of His righteousness.

When we forget this, we turn the Church into a place of judgment. When we do remember, we create space for the guilty to find home again.

We all need this kind of church. Because, if we are honest, we are all guilty of something. And if there is no grace for the guilty, there is no hope for any of us. The gospel is not "clean yourself up and come to Christ." It is "come to Christ, and He will make you new." We must stop expecting people to look healed before they are allowed to enter the hospital.

When Grace Threatens Our Image

If grace offends our sense of justice, it also threatens our image. And in today's media-driven culture, image can be everything.

It is worth asking: what are we most afraid of—the sin itself or the scandal that comes with it? Too often, church leaders act quickly not out of concern for the soul of the fallen but out of fear of what people will say.

Too often, we are more afraid of the scandal than the sin. We scramble to manage optics, while souls bleed quietly in the pews.

Image becomes more important than integrity. Managing perception becomes more urgent than ministering to people.

But the gospel has always been scandalous. Jesus was called a drunkard and a friend of sinners. He hung out with tax collectors, prostitutes, and outcasts. His ministry was filled with risk because it was rooted in grace.

Grace will cost us. It may cost us donors, influence, or status. However, if we are unwilling to pay that price, we must ask whether we are following Christ or merely curating a brand.

Reimagining Church Discipline

A grace-filled church does not ignore sin—it confronts it with truth and love. Discipline should always be restorative, not retributive. Its goal is not to punish but to heal.

Imagine a church where confession is met with care, where failure leads to discipleship, not dismissal. Where the broken are embraced, not shunned. This is not wishful thinking. It is biblical.

Galatians 6:1 says, "Brothers and sisters, if someone is caught in a sin, you who live by the Spirit should restore that person gently. But watch yourselves, or you also may be tempted."

Restore. Gently. With humility. That is the roadmap.

Whether it is a pastor, a small group leader, a friend in crisis, or a teen who strays, our posture should be the same: restore. Gently. Together.

7
Rejection, Not Redemption

> *"The Church is not a museum for saints, but a hospital for sinners."*
> *— attributed to St. Augustine*

There is a moment in every believer's life when they come face-to-face with their own brokenness. In that moment, they have a choice: to hide in shame or to reach for grace. For many, the hope is that the Church—God's own family—will be the hand extended in that dark moment, the embrace that says, "You are still one of us." Too often, the opposite happens. Instead of redemption, what they encounter is rejection.

In this chapter, we look at the ways the Church has often chosen to exile its wounded rather than bind up their wounds. We explore the theology, the fear, and the fractured practices that turn moments of repentance into moments of excommunication. This is not a critique born of bitterness, but of longing—a longing for a Church that looks more like Jesus.

A Legacy of Discarding the Fallen

The early Church faced real dangers. Heresy, moral failure, and betrayal could fracture fragile communities. Even then, the guiding principle of Jesus' ministry was reconciliation. Paul, though often stern, always pointed toward restoration.

"You who are spiritual should restore him gently" (Galatians 6:1 NIV).

"All this is from God, who reconciled us to himself through Christ and gave us the ministry of reconciliation: that God was reconciling the world to himself in Christ, not counting people's sins against them. And he has committed to us the message of reconciliation" (2 Corinthians 5:18-19 NIV)

Over time, fear has somehow taken precedence over faith. Image has taken priority over intimacy. The Church, meant to be a haven, has sometimes become a hall of shame.

We have built communities around the pretense of perfection. We celebrate the polished testimony but shun the messy middle. You have likely heard the testimony that goes something like this: "I was a drug addict and one night I gave my life to Jesus and I have never touched the stuff again." Amazing, but what about those who have been struggling still, long after a salvation experience? We exalt the recovered but ignore those still recovering. Thus, the hurting learn quickly to stay silent or leave.

It happens in subtle ways. A whisper. A cold shoulder. A sudden exclusion from volunteer rosters. Sometimes, it is explicit: a call to step down, a formal removal, a public announcement meant to "preserve the witness" of the church. Still beneath it all is the same message: "Your sin is too visible. Your repentance is too inconvenient."

Today's MIAs: The Disappeared Disciples

Modern churches are filled with invisible absences—the MIAs, the Missing In Action. These are people who once served, sang, gave, led, or taught—until a moment of failure or personal struggle pushed them to the margins or entirely out the door. They did not leave because they stopped believing; they left because they no longer felt a sense of belonging.

Some are divorced and now feel unwelcome. Some have confessed a personal failure and found only distance. Some have dared to question a doctrine, to wrestle publicly with doubt, and found their place on the team quietly removed.

Many of these MIAs were once central to the church's life. Nevertheless, no one calls now. No one asks. No one says, "We miss you."

The Church must wake up to the reality that when we do not offer redemption, we are silently writing people out of the body of Christ.

These MIAs carry wounds that are often invisible but profoundly deep. They walk around with the memory of doors closed, of friendships that cooled, of leadership that turned its back rather than opened its arms. Some try new churches but never quite feel safe enough to be seen. Others leave their faith entirely, not because they have stopped believing in God, but because they have stopped believing they have a place among His people.

These are not minor losses. They are amputations in the body of Christ. If the Church is to be truly whole, it must acknowledge the pain it has caused and commit to the hard, holy work of reconciliation.

The False Economy of Purity

One of the most insidious misconceptions in modern church culture is the notion that purity is something to be achieved through exclusion. We construct barriers around our congregations, not to preserve the sacred, but to protect appearances. The idea that the presence of a repentant sinner somehow jeopardizes the church's integrity reveals a deep confusion about the nature of holiness.

Rejection, Not Redemption

This mentality creates a false economy—one in which we trade people for perception, healing for image control. We begin to value a sanitized narrative over a redemptive one. In doing so, we forget that Christ's very mission was not to call the righteous, but sinners to repentance.

Purity, as taught by Jesus, was never about distance. It was about presence. It was about being in the mess with people, walking with them, bearing their burdens, and restoring them in love. Holiness is not a fragile relic. It is a powerful, active force that transforms the unclean, not by avoidance but by engagement.

Consider the way Jesus conducted Himself. He did not avoid defilement; He ran toward it. He touched the leper. He dined with tax collectors. He defended the adulterous woman. His presence did not compromise His holiness—it demonstrated it.

When the Church loses this posture, it replaces the gospel with a marketing strategy. We begin to manage our brand rather than shepherd our flock. Jesus did not bleed for a brand. He died for His bride, a bride without blemish is not the one who has never been hurt, but the one who has been healed.

To pursue purity without mercy is to miss the gospel entirely. Mercy does not excuse sin; it addresses it with love and the commitment to restoration. The purest communities are not the ones without struggle, but the ones that stay, forgive, and walk each other home.

True holiness is never threatened by brokenness. In fact, it is in the presence of sin that holiness shines most clearly. Jesus did not avoid lepers, prostitutes, or tax collectors—He embraced them. The Church, as His body, should do the same.

Instead, we construct walls. We enforce silence. We send away the hurting to "get right" before they can return. In doing so, we betray our own message.

I recall a time when a brother in Christ and I would drive downtown early on Sundays to pick up a vanload of homeless people. We welcomed them with breakfast, worshiped alongside them, shared lunch, and saw them back home. These were not projects—they became friends.

However, the welcome wore thin. Complaints emerged—about smells, unpredictability, discomfort. No one said they were not welcome. However, tone speaks volumes. A pastor gently pulled us aside: "We are not sure this aligns with our church's direction." Others suggested a downtown ministry might be better suited.

Thus, we stopped. Not because the need disappeared, but because our courage did.

This was not just rejection of the poor. It was a rejection of our calling. Moreover, it revealed how much we, the church, value comfort over communion.

I think of the man who admitted to his pastor that he had relapsed in his pornography use. He was removed from leadership and never followed up on the matter. A man who came seeking help was met with abandonment.

I think of the assistant pastor who made foolish, flirtatious comments online—a moment of lapse, not malice. The response? Immediate dismissal. No conversation. No consideration of past faithfulness. Just exile. Sure, the lead pastor says we never told him and his hurting, bewildered family not to come again, but would you?

Moreover, I think of those we never hear from again. The ones who slip quietly away after being shamed, who stop showing up, who stop believing that grace is for them.

Jesus Stays

In the Gospel accounts, Jesus did not walk away from the broken. Instead, He touched the untouchables, embraced lepers with hands that others recoiled in fear to use. He wept with the mourners, not just offering platitudes but sitting in the ashes of grief with those in pain. He ate with the rejected, not to endorse their behavior but to affirm their worth. Each of these actions was a deliberate

Rejection, Not Redemption

confrontation of religious norms and societal boundaries. He placed Himself among the outcasts, not as a gesture of charity, but as a declaration of love.

When Peter denied Him, Jesus restored him.

When Thomas doubted Him, Jesus invited him to put his finger into the wounds.

When the woman at the well was caught in shame, Jesus offered her living water.

Why then is the Church so quick to walk away?

Perhaps it is fear. Fear of what others will think. Fear of appearing to condone sin.

Fear of losing control; yet the love of Christ casts out fear. The call to bear one another's burdens is not optional.

One core reason for the church's rejection of the fallen is the deep, often unspoken fear of contamination. Like the Pharisees who avoided the leper or the bleeding woman, there remains a belief that those who struggle will somehow corrupt the community. We draw lines not for holiness, but for control. We say, "Stay over there until you are clean," forgetting that Christ crossed every line to bring the outsider in. This fear masquerades as discernment, but it is often little more than self-protection—an unwillingness to let the messiness of redemption stain our pews. We hold others at arm's length to avoid confronting the fact that their struggle reminds us of our own. Thus, we perpetuate a culture of hiding, of silence, of quiet exits instead of loud reconciliations.

Instead, Jesus flipped that on its head. When He touched the unclean, they did not make Him unclean—He made them clean. His holiness was not diminished by contact with sin; it was revealed through it.

Churches must stop treating struggling believers as spiritual biohazards. If the Spirit of Christ lives in us, then we should be the first to approach, not the first to withdraw.

The Need to Belong

At the heart of every act of confession is not just guilt—it is a plea. A vulnerable, trembling whisper that says, "I still want to be part of you. I still want to matter here." Confession is not a performance for punishment; it is an act of hope. It is someone stepping into the light, risking rejection in exchange for the possibility of love, acceptance, and healing.

To respond with silence, with discomfort, or with institutional distance is to speak a devastating word back: "You no longer belong." That is not just organizational policy—it is a spiritual wound. Furthermore, it is not the voice of Christ.

Jesus never responded to vulnerability with coldness. When people brought their brokenness to Him, He did not recoil. He did not draft up behavior contracts. He did not pass the issue off to a subcommittee. He touched lepers. He knelt in the dust with the woman caught in adultery. He wept at Lazarus's tomb. He restored Peter with breakfast by the sea, not a tribunal.

In the parable of the Prodigal Son, Jesus paints a picture of the Father's heart with such shocking grace that it scandalizes the rule-keepers. The father did not wait on the porch with folded arms, demanding an account. He did not set conditions for return. He ran to his son—dirty, disheveled, still smelling of pigs and shame—and embraced him before a single word of apology was spoken. He did not need the perfect confession. He saw the posture of return, and that was enough.

The prodigal's belongings were never really in question to the father. It was only questioned by the older brother—the one who had stayed, but forgot what grace looks like.

How often does the Church behave like that older brother? Suspicious of someone's return. Holding a measuring stick instead of open arms, protecting moral scorecards instead of throwing parties for the found.

Belonging is not earned in the Kingdom—it is inherited. It is offered through grace.

The cross declares it to every prodigal: You still have a place. You are still a son. You are still a daughter.

The Church must learn to run again and embrace—not just metaphorically, but visibly, practically, and consistently. That means pastors who walk with broken members, rather than distancing themselves from them. It means leadership teams who err on the side of mercy rather than image control. It means Sunday gatherings that do not just platform the polished but create space for those still in the wilderness to say, "I am not there yet," and hear, "You still belong."

Belonging heals what shame fractures. It restores what silence suffocates. In a world where many people are yearning for connection, the Church has the opportunity to embody the radical embrace of Jesus—a belonging that precedes change, welcomes the weary, and makes space for sinners still on their way home.

What If We Stayed?

What if, when someone confessed their sin, the Church did not draw back, but leaned in? What if instead of awkward silence or a closed-door meeting, the first response was compassion—visible, vocal, and immediate. Not a hushed prayer whispered behind the scenes, but a community-wide declaration: "You are not alone."

What if confession did not cue distance, but drew people closer?

What if instead of being quietly removed from leadership, the person struggling was assigned a spiritual mentor, a prayer team, a small group that said, "We will walk with you through this." What if healing was seen not as a precondition for inclusion, but as the fruit of belonging?

What if there were a culture where transparency was not punished but honored? Where honesty was not a liability but a doorway into a deeper relationship. A place where people did not have to hide their relapse, their doubts, their marriage struggles, or their mental health battles out of fear of being disqualified from love.

What if the words "I need help" were met with "Thank you for trusting us. Let us walk this together." What if we stopped treating vulnerability as weakness and started seeing it as the courageous first step toward healing?

How many more would come forward if they believed they would not be shamed?

How many more would confess if confession were met with celebration, not because of the sin, but because of the courage to bring it into the light?

How many marriages could be saved? How many lives could be spared from isolation, addiction, or despair? How many prodigals would find their way home sooner if they knew the porch light was still on and the door had not been deadbolted?

What if the Church were known not as the place that punishes the fallen, but as the place that helps them rise?

The truth is, the Church does not lose its witness when it admits brokenness—it loses it when it pretends it is not there. The watching world does not need a polished performance; it needs a redeemed people. A community that shows what happens when grace meets truth in the middle of the mess.

This kind of Church would be messy. It would be unpredictable. It would require time, effort, patience, and the willingness to get our hands dirty. Nevertheless, it would also be beautiful, because it would look a lot more like Jesus.

What if we stayed, even when it got hard? What if we stayed in the conversation instead of canceling the person? What if we stayed in relationship when the easy road was to walk away? Because staying—truly staying—is how people heal. Furthermore, healing, not hiding, is the heart of the gospel.

Our witness to the world is not strengthened by hiding our sin. It is strengthened by showing how we handle it.

Rejection, Not Redemption

A church that only celebrates victory is not honest. A church that walks with the struggling? That shows what grace looks like in the long arc of sanctification? That is compelling.

If we want the world to believe in redemption, we must live it among ourselves.

We need a new imagination. One shaped by the cross, where Jesus did not reject the guilty, but bore their guilt. A church shaped by that cross will not send away the broken—it will bring them in.

This does not mean the absence of standards. It means the presence of mercy. It means the process of restoration is clear, gentle, and rooted in relationship.

It means we say, "There is still a place for you here."

Imagine What Could Be

Imagine a church service where, instead of only polished testimonies of victory, people courageously share their ongoing battles. Where the person wrestling with addiction does not sit alone in silence, but is surrounded by brothers and sisters who will fast, pray, and walk the long road of recovery with them. Where leaders do not fear the loss of their platform if they confess their weariness or wounds—but find a path to healing that is paved with grace, not shame.

Imagine a church culture where every confession is treated as sacred ground.

Where the most honored are not just the ones who "made it through," but those who are in the messy middle and still show up. Where we stop being surprised by sin and start being amazed by grace.

In this church, people do not pretend to be better than they are. They do not smile through gritted teeth while dying inside. They live authentically, speak vulnerably, and forgive lavishly. They sing songs of deliverance—not just in celebration of freedom already won, but in anticipation of freedom still being sought.

Imagine a church where the phrase "you are still one of us" is not rare, but expected.

Where every prodigal is welcomed home with celebration, not suspicion. Where church discipline is not wielded like a weapon but extended as an invitation to restoration, always with clarity, love, and accountability.

This kind of church is not theoretical. It is possible. However, it requires us to unlearn years of image management and relearn the scandalous nature of the gospel. It requires pastors who will prioritize people over performance, elders who will lead from humility, and communities that will choose love over legalism every time.

It demands that we make room—not just for the strong and steady—but for the weak, the wounded, and the wondering. Because it is in making room for them that we rediscover who we are, too.

This is not about being a church that tolerates sin. It is about being a church that ministers to sinners. A church that still believes in the long, sometimes agonizing, always beautiful work of redemption. A church that still believes in miracles—even the quiet, daily ones like a man who stays sober one more day, or a woman who dares to believe that God has not given up on her.

This is the church the world is longing to see. This is the church Jesus is building.

This is the church we must become.

Part II - The Redemptive Cure

8
When the Church Repents

> *"Judgment begins with the household of God." — 1 Peter 4:17 (NIV)*

There's a hush that falls over a room when someone finally admits the truth. You can feel it, the gravity, the release, the crack in the armor. And if that room is holy enough, safe enough, the confession does not lead to condemnation. It leads to healing.

What if the Church, institution, the leadership, the body, made a corporate confession? What if the Church repented? Not just as individuals at an altar, but as a people. As a system. As a culture. What if we stopped managing appearances long enough to admit the truth?

We have made an image an idol. We have weaponized purity. We have abandoned the broken.

We have confused branding with holiness.

We have silenced the doubters and shamed the strugglers.

We have used church discipline to protect reputation instead of restoring the sinner. We have treated Jesus' model of table fellowship with sinners as outdated rather than essential.

We have done it in His name.

What would happen if we stopped defending ourselves long enough to say, "We were wrong"?

The Sound of Repentance

Repentance is not a PR statement. It is not spin. It is not a careful apology written by a legal team. True repentance is raw. Honest. It begins with no defense and ends with no excuses. It is not just the acknowledgment of failure, but also the turning away from it.

Throughout Scripture, God responds to repentance. Nations are spared. Leaders are restored. Communities are healed. However, repentance must always come first.

The Church is not exempt from that divine pattern. If we want to see revival, renewal, restoration, it begins with repentance. And not just from the pews, but from the pulpits, the boards, the councils, the networks, the denominations—and the people who fill them each week. Because while leaders set the tone, congregations sustain the culture.

Imagine this scene: A Sunday morning. A lead pastor takes the pulpit, not to preach, but to confess. "We have not listened. We have not shepherded well. We have chosen silence over courage, reputation over relationship, and control over compassion. We need your forgiveness." Now imagine that across the congregation, there are tears, not from shame, but from relief. Because someone finally said it. Someone finally made it safe again.

This is not fiction. It is possible.

A Theology of Corporate Confession

In Nehemiah 9, the people of Israel stood together, read the Law, and confessed, not only their own sins but the sins of their ancestors. They wore sackcloth. They named the failures of leadership. They recounted the ways God had been faithful and they had not.

This was not self-flagellation. It was cleansing.

The modern Church rarely practices this kind of collective confession. We fear the legal liability, the reputational cost, the loss of donor trust. Instead, we should fear more deeply what happens when we do not repent.

When the Church confesses corporately, we say with our actions: "God, we want to be clean more than we want to be admired."

That kind of humility invites revival.

That kind of posture invites the presence of God.

We have seen glimpses of this kind of humility before: when the Southern Baptist Convention acknowledged its failures in handling abuse, when churches across traditions began confessing their complicity in racial injustice, and more recently, as the historic abuse of Indigenous peoples by Christian institutions has come to light, some churches and denominations have begun issuing public apologies, committing to restitution, and listening to survivors. These moments are imperfect and incomplete, but they matter.

They show that institutions can confess—and when they do, healing becomes possible.

Trading Image for Integrity

Image is about perception. Integrity is about substance. Somewhere along the way, the Church in the West became obsessed with brand management. We created logos, slogans, sermon series graphics, influencer pastors, and curated aesthetics. None of these are evil in themselves, but when image eclipses authenticity, the Church loses its prophetic voice.

In Matthew 23, Jesus said to the Pharisees, "You clean the outside of the cup and dish, but inside they are full of greed and self-indulgence." That same critique rings in the halls of churches today. Too many churches are spotless on the outside and septic on the inside.

Repentance requires that we trade the polished image for something deeper: the integrity to admit where we have failed and the courage to live in the tension of not having it all figured out.

Repentance as Witness

The world is not asking the Church to be perfect. It is asking the Church to be honest.

One of the greatest witnesses the Church could offer today is not a slick video campaign or a well-branded series; it is a sincere apology. It is a community of believers willing to look each other in the eye and say, "I have been part of the problem. Let us be part of the healing."

We often say, "God can use anyone." However, we act like He can only use those who never stumble. We say, "Everyone is welcome," but then exile the wounded when they become inconvenient.

Repentance says, "We were wrong, but we want to do better. And here is how."

That kind of humility disarms cynicism. It softens hard hearts. It says: You are not crazy. We see it too, and we are not okay with staying this way.

A Church That Models What It Preaches

If we preach grace, we must practice grace.

If we preach truth, we must live in the truth, including the truth of our failings.

A repentant Church is not a weak Church. It is a powerful one. Because power does not lie in appearance, it lies in the Spirit. Moreover, the Spirit draws near to the brokenhearted, not the self-assured.

When a Church repents, it becomes a safe place again; a place where people dare to come home. A place where the prodigal finds the porch light still on. A place where the wounded do not have to earn their way back. They just have to show up.

The First Step

No church reforms itself overnight.

No culture of secrecy and shame can be transformed in a single meeting. We must acknowledge that every journey begins with one step.

For some churches, that step is a public confession.

For others, it is a private meeting of leaders deciding to rewrite the playbook.

For others still, it may be listening—really listening—to those who have left, those who were wounded, those who were told they no longer belonged.

The Church does not need a new strategy. It needs a new spirit.

That spirit begins with repentance.

9
The Culture of Grace

In many churches today, grace is treated like a rare pardon—offered in exceptional cases, cautiously extended, and often wrapped in disclaimers to avoid the appearance of being "soft on sin." It is dispensed reactively, not proactively. Reserved for crisis, rather than embedded in culture.

The gospel tells a different story. Grace is not the exception. It is the posture of God toward us—consistent, undeserved, and fierce in love. Grace is not an interruption of justice, but its fulfillment through mercy. It is not permission to sin, but power to overcome it; and more than anything, it is the assurance that we are not abandoned in the struggle.

If grace is the posture of God, then it must become the posture of His Church. Not a backup plan. Not a whispered rescue for the few who confess well enough. Grace must become the default setting of our hearts, our systems, and our communities.

Jesus never made grace contingent on worthiness. He extended it to the undeserving, the weary, the brokenhearted. From the woman at the well to the thief on the cross, every interaction declared this: God's mercy meets us where we are, not where we should have been.

The Culture of Grace

To create a culture of grace, churches must unlearn habits of suspicion and performance. We must let go of the fear that grace leads to compromise. It does not. What leads to compromise is secrecy, shame, and a performance-driven approach to religion. Grace is not soft on sin; it is fierce in love. It is the only force strong enough to confront sin without condemning the sinner.

This begins with those who influence the tone—leaders, yes, but also those in the pews, in small groups, and in everyday relationships. When pastors lead from humility, when elders confess openly, and when people in the congregation normalize grace by the way they listen and forgive, a new tone is set. It says: This is a place for the real you. Not the curated you. Not the social media version of you. The honest, flawed, still-being-formed version of you.

Grace as posture means designing church structures that expect brokenness, not to glorify it, but to minister to it. It means organizing care teams, small groups, and leadership development with an understanding that people are on a journey, not a pedestal. The church does not become less holy when it embraces the messy. It becomes more Christlike.

If we say grace is central to the gospel, then grace must become central to our culture. That will only happen if we teach it, embody it, and build systems around it.

Stories That Shape Culture: Testimony, Transparency, and Truth

Culture is not formed by doctrine alone. It is formed by the stories we tell, the examples we elevate, and the narratives we repeat. What we celebrate becomes what we expect.

Churches often tell testimonies that end with a clean bow. A person was addicted, then they met Jesus, and now they are free. A marriage was in crisis, but then they started attending church, and now it is restored. These stories are true, and they deserve to be celebrated. But they are not the whole truth.

What about the man who is still wrestling with addiction, but has chosen not to isolate anymore?

What about the woman who has not received full healing, but finds strength each week to show up in community?

What about the teenager who does not have all the answers, but trusts that Jesus will hold them through their doubt?

These are also testimonies—ongoing, unresolved, and yet holy. A culture of grace makes room for stories still in progress.

Transparency is not a liability; it is a gift. When someone shares their present-tense struggle, they are offering the community a window into authentic faith. It may be messy. It may be awkward. Nevertheless, it is real, and it is what people need to see.

Jesus never required people to have their affairs in order before approaching Him. He simply asked them to come.

Moreover, truth, when spoken in love, becomes a powerful tool of grace. A grace-shaped church does not shy away from hard conversations. However, it also refuses to turn those conversations into interrogations. Truth is not a weapon in a grace culture; it is a lifeline. It is the rope we throw to one another when we are sinking.

Imagine church services where the platform is not reserved for the polished, but is open to the honest. Imagine small groups where confession is a rhythm, not a surprise. Imagine leadership teams where repentance flows from the top down, not just the bottom up.

We become what we celebrate. If we celebrate transparency, we will become a transparent people. If we celebrate perseverance, we will become a resilient people. If we celebrate grace, we will become a gracious church.

The Culture of Grace

Making Confession Safe Again

Confession used to be a sacred rhythm in the Church. Today, it is a rare and risky venture. Not because sin has disappeared, but because safety has.

Across centuries, Christians have practiced confession in various forms—some through liturgical rites, such as the confessional booth, while others have done so through spontaneous prayer or personal conversations. Nevertheless, at its heart, confession is not about the method. It is about the moment someone says, "I need help," and they are met with grace instead of judgment.

It might happen in a sanctuary, in a living room, or over coffee. It might sound like "I was wrong," or "I am struggling," or "I cannot do this alone." Whatever the form, real confession is a holy risk—an act of trust that the Church will hold what is shared with mercy.

For many, to confess in the Church is to risk exile. Thus, we learn to pretend. We smile in the lobby while our hearts break in silence. We post victories on social media while hiding defeats in solitude. However, we need to remember that what hides in the dark grows in the dark.

Scripture never envisioned a solitary, silent healing. James tells us, "Confess your sins to one another and pray for one another, that you may be healed." (James 5:16)

Confession is not just about forgiveness; it is about healing. However, healing can only happen when confession is received with grace.

Making confession safe again means more than saying, "You are welcome to be honest." It means showing that honesty will not be punished. It means training leaders and members alike in spiritual hospitality—the ability to sit with someone's story, to listen without panic, to pray without performance.

Communion: A Grace-Filled Table

Nowhere is the culture of grace more beautifully enacted than in the act of communion. Nevertheless, even here, we often individualize what was meant to be communal.

The Lord's Supper is not a private moment of silent guilt. It is a public, embodied declaration that we all need grace—together. It is not a table for the worthy; it is a table for the willing. Those who are willing to examine, confess, repent, and receive.

Paul writes in 1 Corinthians 11, "Let a person examine himself, then having done so, let them eat of the bread and drink of the cup." This examination was never meant to create exclusion—it was meant to prepare hearts for shared inclusion.

Communion is not a test; it is a table. At this table, we remember not only what Christ has done, but what He is doing now. He is reconciling us to Himself and each other.

Imagine if churches used the Lord's Supper as a regular opportunity to practice grace:

A time to confess not only to God, but to each other.

A time to forgive old wounds and open new paths of reconciliation.

A time when the brokenness of the body is acknowledged, but so is its healing.

What if, before receiving the elements, we turned to one another and said, "You are still one of us?"

What if communion was not just a ritual of remembrance, but a rhythm of restoration?

The act of breaking bread together should echo the grace that was broken open for us on the cross. In a grace culture, communion becomes more than memory. It becomes ministry.

If communion becomes ministry—if grace is practiced not just in sermons but at the table—then something begins to shift. Over time, the rhythms of grace seep into our culture. It becomes less about moments of mercy and more about the atmosphere we carry. Instead, it becomes a way of being together.

The Air We Breathe

In the end, grace must become more than a doctrine. It must become the air we breathe.

A church where grace is a culture will be a place where people risk being known, where they are not shamed for their needs, but honored for their honesty, where sanctification is not a race to perfection, but a shared walk of persistence.

This kind of culture is not created overnight. It is forged over time, through stories told, systems shaped, leaders formed, and the Spirit moving freely.

It must start somewhere. It starts when we say:

Grace is our posture.

Honesty is our language.

Confession is our rhythm.

Communion is our table.

Love is our covering.

Let the Church become what Christ has always intended it to be: a hospital for sinners. A place not of pretense, but of peace. Not of exclusion, but of embrace.

Let us become a grace-formed people.

10
From Control to Compassion

When Jesus walked the earth, He confronted the religious systems not simply for their rules but for the heart beneath them. The Pharisees and teachers of the law had become gatekeepers of God's presence, deciding who was in and who was out, who was clean and who was not. In doing so, they exchanged compassion for control.

This temptation has not vanished. In many modern churches, control masquerades as spiritual authority. Leadership becomes about maintaining order, preserving the image, and enforcing boundaries, rather than shepherding hearts.

The gospel is not built on control. It is built on freedom—freedom that comes from grace, from truth, and from the indwelling Spirit of God. The role of church leadership, then, is not to tighten the reins but to open the gates. To lead not with coercion, but with compassion.

Control-driven churches often emerge in response to fear:

Fear of losing influence.
Fear of theological error.
Fear of messy situations and scandal.
Fear of being exposed.

From Control to Compassion

Fear of losing influence is one of the most complex and misunderstood dynamics in church leadership. In today's competitive religious landscape, where churches exist on nearly every corner and where attendance often dictates financial stability, pastors can feel immense pressure to grow. This pressure often translates into performance metrics: bodies in seats, programs offered, and dollars raised. When influence is tied to visibility and perceived success, leaders may begin to tighten control to protect the brand of their ministry. The tragic irony is that in trying to preserve relevance and increase reach, churches risk trading away the very authenticity that makes the gospel compelling.

Influence gained through control is fragile; influence anchored in grace endures.

Fear of theological error also plays a major role. Leaders who fear deviation may err toward rigidity, believing strict doctrinal policing will ensure orthodoxy. Doctrine divorced from grace becomes legalism. While truth matters deeply, when truth is enforced without love, it crushes rather than convicts. Compassion does not abandon theological clarity; it deepens it by expressing truth relationally. Jesus embodied truth and grace perfectly—not by diminishing doctrine, but by making it accessible to the broken.

Fear of messy situations and scandal can paralyze a church. With today's digital landscape, one bad headline or viral post can wreak havoc on a church's reputation. In response, some leaders prioritize damage control over disciple care. They adopt risk-averse strategies, withdraw from morally complex scenarios, or swiftly remove people to protect their image. However, messiness is where ministry lives. Jesus entered the homes of sinners, touched lepers, and sat with the demon-afflicted. He did not shy away from the complicated. Neither should we. Scandals do not destroy churches—secrecy and spin do. Compassion brings sin into the light not for spectacle, but for healing. It honors the integrity of the gospel by letting redemption be visible.

Finally, fear of being exposed might be the most personal of all. Many church leaders struggle with their own pain, temptation, or exhaustion. They fear that if they show weakness, their authority will be questioned. So they lead from masks. However, people do not need perfect leaders—they need honest ones. A compassionate church creates space for pastors and elders to be human. It replaces performance with presence, giving leaders permission to confess, rest, and receive care.

However, this fear not only affects leaders. It trickles down into pews, small groups, and family conversations, where grace becomes guarded and honesty feels unsafe. When the goal becomes behavior management rather than heart transformation, the church ceases to reflect Jesus. Furthermore, when leaders define success as uniformity instead of unity, we forget the diversity of gifts and stories that God uses to build His Kingdom.

Jesus did not control His disciples. He invited them. He corrected them. He served them. Moreover, He entrusted His mission to them, even though they had a long way to go.

Compassion as a Leadership Posture

Compassion is not a soft alternative to conviction; it is the expression of Christ's conviction through His character. His compassion was not just reactive; it was invitational. He did not wait for the broken to clean up—He called them near.

He saw the sick, touched the untouchable, and welcomed the outcast without hesitation. His tears were not signs of weakness—they were signs of divine investment. When Jesus wept at Lazarus's tomb, He did so knowing resurrection was moments away. His grief was not for Himself; it was for those who were hurting.

This posture of compassion does not begin and end with leadership—it shapes how congregants speak to one another, how small group leaders respond to confession, and how families reflect the mercy of Christ in their homes.

True spiritual authority flows not from a title but from a towel. The One with all power stooped to wash feet. The King of kings did not claim His rights but laid them down. In a grace-formed church, leadership is not about elevation; it is about descent. Influence is not claimed; it is given away in service.

Building Structures That Heal

For compassion to shape a community, it must be built into its structures, not just its sermons. Systems that reflect grace help a church carry its values into moments of crisis, failure, and deep need. Without compassionate structures, good intentions collapse under pressure.

In a grace-shaped church, restorative discipline is not reactive punishment; it is redemptive engagement. When someone sins or stumbles, the goal is not image control or swift removal but restoration through relationship. Churches must revisit how Matthew 18 is practiced, not as a courtroom process but as a pathway of healing. It is not about stacking witnesses to prove guilt; it is about surrounding the fallen with people who are committed to their return.

Honest confession must be safe again. Whether it is in an elder meeting, a small group, or a private conversation, believers must know they will not be discarded for telling the truth. A church shaped by grace equips its people to walk alongside the repentant, rather than standing in judgment over them. We need language and posture that reflects mercy, not suspicion. This includes developing leadership teams that model confession themselves, showing that grace is not a reward for the strong but a refuge for the honest.

Mental health support should also be integrated, not outsourced. A grace-filled church understands that spiritual and emotional well-being are deeply connected. It creates space for rest, for counseling, and for grief. The church does not need to replace professional help, but it must stop pretending that prayer alone addresses every wound. Churches that heal recognize trauma, acknowledge depression, and walk patiently with those who suffer.

A grace-shaped church does not just expect these systems from leaders—it becomes a community that practices them in daily life: forgiving quickly, listening deeply, and resisting the urge to cancel or control one another.

Leadership That Shares the Load

Leadership in a grace-shaped church is not about charisma or command—it is about shared responsibility. When leadership is distributed among elders, pastors, deacons, or lay ministers, it creates a culture where no one carries the spiritual weight alone. The burdens of care are shared, wisdom is multiplied, and accountability becomes mutual.

This is not just a leadership strategy; it is a discipleship model. It invites people into ownership, maturity, and relational ministry. The early church thrived not because of a singular, star leader, but because Spirit-filled men and women operated as a body, with each part doing its work.

Shared leadership also resists the gravitational pull of celebrity culture. In a world obsessed with platforms, churches must prize presence. The pastor is not the brand; Christ is. When churches center around a personality, they risk collapsing when that personality falters. However, when shepherding is shared, and no one voice dominates the room, the church becomes less fragile and more faithful.

Shared leadership affirms the full community. It welcomes diverse gifts, theological insights, and perspectives. It makes space for the young and the seasoned, the bold and the quiet. It replaces hierarchy with humility and creates a leadership ecosystem where compassion, not control, is the currency.

Jesus: The Compassionate Shepherd

Ultimately, the shift from control to compassion is not a strategy; it is a transformation. It is a return to Christ.

Jesus described Himself as the Good Shepherd. Not a manager. Not a warden. A shepherd—one who knows His sheep, calls them by name, and lays down His life for them. He did not drive them with fear. He led them with love. He did not control with rules; He guided with relationship.

In ancient times, shepherds were not part of society's upper class. They were rough-skinned laborers, often overlooked, spending long, isolated stretches in the field. Their work was not clean or glamorous; it was intimate, sacrificial, and relentless. They did not rule from a distance; they lived with the flock. Ate beside them. Slept near them. Fought off danger to protect them. When a sheep went missing, the shepherd did not send someone else, but he went himself. Through valleys. Over rocks. Into shadows. The shepherd's worth was not found in appearance or position, but in the well-being of his sheep.

Jesus embodied that kind of leadership.

He did not shame Peter when he failed. He made him breakfast and asked him to feed others.

He did not chastise Thomas for doubting. He offered His wounds as proof, meeting him in his skepticism with grace.

He did not rebuke Martha for her grief. He entered it with her. He wept. He did not condemn the woman with a past. He gave her a future.

Furthermore, when He looked over Jerusalem, knowing they would reject Him, He still cried: "How often I have longed to gather your children together, as a hen gathers her chicks under her wings, and you were not willing." Matthew 23:37 (NIV)

This is not a leader obsessed with being right. This is a Savior grieved by lost relationship.

Jesus' compassion did not cancel truth—it fulfilled it. He did not lower the bar of holiness; He lifted people into it with His love. He modeled a kind of strength that stooped, a kind of authority that knelt to wash feet.

He embraced the broken. He touched the unclean. He stood silent before His accusers, not to protect Himself, but to fulfill the mission of mercy.

If the Church is to reflect Christ, then we must reclaim this kind of shepherding. Not the kind that guards image, but the kind that pursues the one who wandered. Not the kind that draws lines to keep people out, but the kind that crosses boundaries to bring people in.

To lead like Jesus is to live among the sheep, not above them. To measure our value not by numbers or image, but by how well the vulnerable are protected, how the wounded are healed, and how the lost are restored.

That is the heart of our Savior. It must become the heart of His Church.

The Table and the Towel

One of the clearest indicators of whether a church is built on control or compassion is how it handles the Lord's Table.

In churches of control, communion becomes a test: Are you worthy enough to participate? The table becomes a checkpoint, a place to measure one's worth, a ritualized gate of exclusion.

In churches of compassion, communion becomes an invitation: Do you know you need grace? The table becomes a reminder that none of us earned our seats. We are not guests of honor—we are beggars who need to be fed.

Paul's instruction in 1 Corinthians 11 is often misunderstood. He calls the church to examine itself, not to disqualify the broken, but to prevent hypocrisy. The problem was not that people were taking communion unworthily because they were sinners; rather, it was that they were doing so with division in their hearts, disregarding the unity and humility the table represents.

Communion is not about personal piety. It is about shared grace. The bread is broken for all. The cup is poured for all. When we receive it together, we are declaring—not our righteousness—but Christ's.

Imagine communion that includes:
- Moments of shared confession, where we admit our need before God and each other.
- An opportunity to extend forgiveness, even across the aisle, before receiving the elements.
- A pastoral reminder that grace, not guilt, is what makes this table possible.

Imagine if communion became not just a symbol of remembrance, but a practice of reconciliation.

In the earliest Church, the Lord's Supper was not a monthly ritual. It was central. It was a meal, a gathering, a holy collision of broken people and boundless grace. It was where division dissolved, where unity was visible. Where mercy had flavor, and forgiveness had texture.

Furthermore, just as central as the bread and the cup were the basin and the towel. On the night Jesus was betrayed, He did not just break bread—He bent low. He washed feet. He taught that communion was not only about remembrance, but about humility. About serving one another as He served us.

It was a meal, a moment, a reminder: We are one. We are broken.

Furthermore, we are being made whole together, not just at the table, but at the towel.

What a Compassionate Church Looks Like

A compassionate church trains leaders to be present, not perfect.

It recognizes that authenticity is better than polish. Leaders are encouraged to bring their full selves—wounds, questions, and all—into ministry. They model vulnerability and invite others to do the same. This breaks the illusion that pastors and elders are spiritual superheroes, allowing real discipleship to occur.

It structures its practices around people, not performance.

Metrics like attendance and giving do not define the mission. Instead, the church asks, 'Are people being healed here?' Are they growing in grace? Are they known, loved, and equipped?

Programs are tools, not trophies. The measure of success becomes the depth of care, not the flash of presentation.

It sees failure as a beginning, not an ending.

When someone stumbles, the response is not exile but embrace. The question is not, 'How could you?' but 'How can we help you back up?' Grace becomes a launchpad for restoration, not a loophole for shame. The church commits to walking with people, not walking away from them.

It treats confession as sacred, not scandalous.

Testimonies are not reserved for the already resolved. In this church, confession is not a surprise; it is a rhythm. It is honored as a courageous step toward light. There is no rush to fix or silence the confessor, just a quiet, steady commitment to walk alongside.

It resists the urge to hide behind image and embraces the call to be a hospital for sinners. Rather than polishing a brand, it embraces brokenness as a badge of belonging. It is unafraid of messiness because Jesus was never afraid of mess. The image it protects is not its own but Christ's—reflected in compassion, mercy, and truth.

This kind of church will not always be neat. It will not win the approval of those who prize certainty and control. However, it will be a place where prodigals come home. Where doubters find welcome. Where the weary are not worked harder but held closer. It will be a church that reflects the likeness of Jesus.

The Road Ahead

Shifting from control to compassion will cost us. It will cost pride. It will cost the illusion of order. Nevertheless, it will lead us into love.

From Control to Compassion

Control builds walls. Compassion opens doors. Control protects power—compassion shares it.

If the Church is to become what Christ died to make her, then we must relinquish control, not responsibility, not wisdom, but the image-obsessed fear that keeps people outside the gate.

Compassion is not a suggestion. It is the calling of every follower of Christ.

Let us choose it. Let us embody it. Let us build it—brick by gracious brick—until the Church reflects the compassion of the One who called her beloved.

A grace-formed church leads with humility, welcomes the broken, and multiplies compassion. It refuses to control. It chooses to serve.

The world does not need another religious brand. It needs people who live the mercy they preach.

May we become those people. May we offer our tables. May we pick up the towel.

11
Discipleship That Heals

From Cookie-Cutter Christianity to Christlike Community

One of the most damaging myths in modern discipleship is the notion that Christian maturity means looking, acting, and thinking alike. We often equate spiritual growth with uniformity: same books, same answers, same tone, same image. This creates a kind of factory model of faith—what some have called "cookie-cutter Christianity."

This model is appealing because it is measurable. If everyone is reading the same book, attending the same study, and parroting the same answers, then spiritual formation feels efficient. However, it is counterfeit. It values compliance over transformation, behavior over belonging.

One size does not fit all. When we try to force every believer into the same mold, we do not produce unity—we produce misfits who feel they are failing simply for being different.

When I was once asked by a pastor what discipleship meant to me, my gut reaction was deeply negative. Why? Because I had been part of what I now recognize as micromanaged discipleship. Everyone was expected to read the same material. Discussion was rigidly guided. If you did not answer the "right" way—or worse, did not feel safe to answer at all—you were seen as unsubmitted, unspiritual, and rebellious.

This is not what Christ intended.

Jesus did not call people into a discipleship of duplication. He called them into life with Him. Peter did not look like John. Mary Magdalene did not minister in the same way as Joanna. Thomas's questions were not a threat to Jesus—they were a bridge to trust.

The Church must move away from discipleship models that elevate conformity and embrace a community that celebrates Christlikeness in its diverse forms. A Christlike community does not demand sameness—it cultivates depth.

Mentorship, Not Micromanagement

True discipleship is not about managing someone's spiritual performance. It is about walking with them in real time, in real life. It is about seeing the person, not the program. Programs can serve as on-ramps, but they must never replace presence.

While attending The Upper Room in Minneapolis, I witnessed one of the most effective mentorship programs I have ever seen. Adults from the congregation volunteered to mentor youth, but not in the traditional top-down, lecture-heavy way. After screening, each mentor participated in a speed-dating-style event where they met and talked with each of the teens interested in mentorship. Once paired, they became friends, deeply involved in one another's lives.

These were not accountability partners checking up on reading plans. They were human beings investing in one another's growth. Mentors attended their mentees' sports games, helped shop for prom outfits, took walks, and had coffee. The mentees, in turn, participated in the lives of their mentors. It was not one-sided. It was mutual.

What emerged from that structure was not compliance—it was trust. Several of those relationships lasted far beyond the formal program. They were built on time, presence, love, and a long view of spiritual growth.

This is what discipleship should be.

Jesus did not follow a rigid curriculum with His disciples. He did not hand them a syllabus or schedule a six-week growth track. He lived among them. He ate with them, prayed with them, told them stories, asked thoughtful questions, and shared the rhythms of ordinary life. He corrected them gently when they were off course and stood by them when they stumbled. That is not a program—that is presence. That is mentorship. That is spiritual parenting.

Jesus did not sit His disciples down and announce, "Today, we are learning how to pray." Instead, He modeled a life so rich in communion with the Father that the disciples could not help but ask, "Lord, teach us to pray." His method was not instruction-first, but relationship-first. He waited for their hunger to surface, for their curiosity to be stirred, and then He responded—not with lectures, but with lived example.

Discipleship at its best is not a mandate to follow a script. It is an invitation to walk together, to ask real questions, to live in such a way that spiritual hunger awakens naturally and is met with wisdom, grace, and companionship.

Creating Safe, Accountable Spiritual Friendships

Not every Christian relationship needs to be labeled "discipleship" to be powerful. Sometimes, the most transformational relationships are friendships rooted in Christ, saturated in grace, and committed to mutual growth and development.

However, for these relationships to thrive, churches must foster a culture where vulnerability is not perceived as dangerous, where confession is not equated with failure. Where spiritual conversations happen over dinner tables, not just behind pulpits.

A healing model of discipleship nurtures spaces where people can say:

"I am struggling with doubt."
"I feel stuck."
"I am afraid to be honest."
Then they hear in response: "I am still with you."
That is where healing begins.

This kind of safety does not remove accountability; it strengthens it. When people are secure in their belonging, they are more likely to receive truth in love. When discipleship is rooted in relationship, correction feels like care rather than condemnation.

In Paul's letters, we see him refer to those he mentors not as subordinates, but as children, siblings, and friends. This familial language speaks volumes. Discipleship that heals is discipleship that loves.

A New Vision for Formation

Imagine a church where spiritual formation was less about filling out booklets and more about bearing one another's burdens, where the goal was not to clone the leader but to cultivate the unique work of Christ in each person, where mentoring was not about spiritual superiority but about faithful friendship.

This is the invitation of discipleship that heals: not to produce polished performers but to raise up honest, grace-formed followers of Jesus.

Not everyone is ready for deep friendship right away. That is okay. However, every disciple needs someone who sees them. Someone who will stay. Someone who does not just check their box, but carries their story. That is the kind of discipleship that changes lives.

Practical Steps to Developing Discipleship

Discipleship is not a program to be implemented but a culture to be cultivated. Churches can create environments where discipleship flourishes by focusing on relationship, rhythm, and realism. These are suggestions—not a script:

Start Small and Personal

Begin with intentional relationships rather than large-scale programs. Invite a few individuals into regular, purposeful connection. Ask, 'Who is someone I can walk with in faith over the next year?'

Create Meal-Based Groups

Shared meals have always been a powerful context for discipleship. Jesus often taught over food. Churches can organize meal groups or small gatherings that meet regularly for food, conversation, prayer, and support. The table becomes a sacred space for sharing stories and offering spiritual encouragement.

Designate Mentorship Circles

Encourage experienced believers to commit to a season of walking with one or two younger believers. Provide training, not as control, but as encouragement for how to listen well, ask good questions, and live transparently.

Normalize Everyday Spiritual Conversations

Discipleship thrives when spiritual life is not compartmentalized. Encourage conversations about Scripture, doubt, calling, and everyday holiness to happen in normal rhythms—during errands, while exercising, or over coffee.

Utilize Mixed-Age and Cross-Cultural Pairings

Diversity enriches discipleship. Encourage pairings and small groups that reflect different ages, ethnic backgrounds, and life experiences. Each participant brings a piece of God's image to the table. Do not forget the children. Even young children can benefit from interactions with adults outside of their parents.

Celebrate Milestones

Recognize growth moments: baptisms, answered prayers, breakthroughs in understanding or obedience. Celebrating publicly affirms progress and reminds the community of God's ongoing work.

Encourage Feedback and Flexibility

Every discipleship effort should include space to reflect on what is working and what is not. Some structures may need to change to fit the people, rather than the other way around.

Above all, remember that discipleship is not about getting people to do church things. It is about helping people become more like Jesus, right where they are. A practical, relational culture of grace leads to a discipleship model that is sustainable, adaptable, and Christ-centered.

The Journey Together

Discipleship was never meant to be a factory line of spiritual clones—it was always intended to be a journey of transformation, shaped by relationship, grounded in grace, and responsive to the unique story God is writing in each life. When we move away from micromanagement and performance-based models, we make space for a kind of growth that lasts: the kind rooted in love, honesty, and presence.

Discipleship that heals does not rush. It does not demand perfection. It walks beside, listens well, speaks truth with tenderness, and remains when others would retreat.

In a world of quick fixes and shallow faith, the Church is called to something deeper—to raise up disciples who are not just informed, but formed; not just managed, but mentored; not just shaped by programs, but transformed by presence.

Let us build that kind of discipleship.

The kind that Jesus lived.

The kind that changes everything.

12
The Ministry of Restoration

Restoration Begins with Grace

Restoration is not damage control; it is discipleship in its most redemptive form. Churches often excel at calling people to repentance but struggle to walk with them after they have done so. This chapter explores how to restore, not just remove, those who fall, in a way that reflects the heart of Christ.

What Restoration Really Means

Restoration is more than a second chance—it is the spiritual reweaving of a person back into the fabric of community and mission. In too many churches, restoration is reduced to waiting out a sentence. A fallen believer, especially a leader, is removed from their role, given a vague and lonely season of waiting, and left to prove they are safe again. However, that is not biblical restoration. Biblical restoration is not passive—it is purposeful. It involves intentional community, spiritual care, and a goal of re-commissioning, not just rehabilitation.

In Galatians 6:1, Paul urges the church: "If someone is caught in a sin, you who live by the Spirit should restore that person gently." The word "restore" here is the same word used for mending a net or setting a broken bone. It implies a hands-on, skilled, and careful process, not just avoidance until the pain goes away.

Jesus and the Breakfast of Redemption

The goal of restoration is always reintegration, not erasure. It seeks to preserve dignity, protect the flock, and help the fallen rediscover their calling, now seasoned by humility. Jesus restored Peter not by handing him a ministry manual, but by meeting him over breakfast, naming the failure, and re-inviting him into leadership: "Feed my sheep." This model—graceful, direct, and deeply relational—must shape how we respond when those among us fall, not with a checklist, but with compassion, accountability, and a deep hope for renewal.

Establishing a Restoration Framework

Restoration is never a one-size-fits-all formula, but it does require intentionality, structure, and care. Churches that wish to practice redemptive discipline must prepare themselves in advance of the crisis. Having a clearly defined and biblically grounded restoration framework—agreed upon by leadership and communicated as part of the church's culture—allows the process to function with integrity when failure occurs.

A restoration plan is not just a leadership tool—it is a communal safeguard. When a church has already articulated how it restores the fallen, it removes guesswork in the midst of emotional, high-stakes moments. It also helps the congregation understand why certain things are being said—or not being said. It maintains transparency without violating confidentiality. In this way, the church avoids the ditches of secrecy on one side and spectacle on the other.

Perhaps most importantly, a pre-established process provides reassurance to those who have fallen. It communicates that they will not be subjected to impulsive decisions or treated as liabilities to be managed. Instead, they will be cared for thoughtfully, prayerfully, and redemptively. Knowing that a path of restoration exists—and that it is rooted in love, not shame—can be the first step toward healing for someone who has fallen.

The plan should remain flexible enough to accommodate individual circumstances yet structured enough to provide a consistent path forward. Restoration without a path feels arbitrary. Restoration without discretion can feel unsafe for both the individual being restored and the community observing.

What follows is a practical outline churches can adapt to their context—one that holds truth and grace together and points every step toward healing, not hiding.

13

Step 1: When Truth Breaks the Silence
Acknowledgment and Ownership

The road to restoration begins with truth. No healing can happen until the fallen person acknowledges what went wrong and takes full ownership of it. This step is foundational—not because it satisfies public curiosity or appeases leadership, but because healing begins where honesty begins. Without ownership, there can be no repentance. Moreover, without repentance, there can be no restoration.

Acknowledgment is not merely admitting what happened; it is taking personal responsibility without deflection, minimization, or blame-shifting. "I made a mistake" is not enough. True ownership says, "I sinned. I caused harm. I take full responsibility."

This does not mean every detail must be made public. However, it does mean the individual must come to a place of honest self-confrontation. Often, this happens best in private, sacred conversations with pastoral mentors or spiritual counselors before any public statements are made.

At the same time, safe spaces for confession are crucial. If a church culture punishes honesty or rushes to discipline before listening, people will hide. Fear drives secrecy.

Compassionate leadership creates an environment where confession is not coerced but invited—where a fallen believer can say, "I need help," and know they will be heard, not humiliated.

It is also important that leaders resist the temptation to extract confession for the sake of optics. The goal is not image control, but soul care. Forced apologies, especially when driven by PR concerns or social pressure, often produce shallow remorse without lasting change. True confession cannot be manufactured; it must be surrendered.

Pastors, elders, and restoration teams must take the posture of shepherds, not prosecutors. When someone begins to own their story, the church's job is not to tighten the spotlight, but to hold the lantern, offering enough light to walk forward in truth without being scorched by shame.

In short: confession must be invited, not demanded; nurtured, not managed. When it comes from the heart, it opens the door to a kind of grace that transforms.

Sincerity is the soul of confession.

What makes acknowledgment redemptive is not just the words spoken, but the spirit in which they are offered. A sincere confession is not calculated or performative, but contrite. It does not aim to control outcomes or avoid consequences, but to be known in truth. When confession is sincere, it becomes fertile ground for grace to grow.

However, not all admissions are equal. Deflection often masquerades as confession.

Leaders should watch for warning signs, such as:
- Language that shifts blame onto circumstances or other people.
- Appeals to how "hard things have been lately" instead of addressing sin directly.
- Emotional performances that seem rehearsed or disproportionately self-pitying.
- A rush to restore image rather than rebuild trust.

A genuine confession does not flinch from the truth—it steps into the light, no matter the cost.

Practical Markers of True Acknowledgment

When someone is sincerely acknowledging their failure, look for:
- Specific language of repentance: "I sinned," not vague regrets.
- Ownership without excuses, comparisons, or deflection.
- A focus on those harmed, not personal image repair.
- Willingness to listen, submit to care, and walk through consequences.
- A posture of humility—asking for help, not control.

Remember, repentance does not come quickly or easily. It is fostered in an environment of grace. It takes time. David did not repent from his sin until the prophet confronted him.

14
Step 2: Care Before Control
Immediate Care and Containment

When a moral or spiritual failure comes to light—whether involving someone in leadership or sitting in the pew—our first instinct must not be image protection or public relations. It must be careful, real, and immediate pastoral care for everyone affected.

This step begins with two simultaneous goals: (1) providing compassionate care for the individuals involved, and (2) containing the situation responsibly without covering it up. These two aims are not at odds. In fact, when handled wisely, they support one another.

In many cases, a temporary removal from roles of public ministry, influence, service, or even worship participation may be appropriate—not as punishment, but as a necessary boundary. It allows space for reflection, healing, and care. Nevertheless, removal from public ministry should not mean removal from community. Too often, churches cut people off in the name of protection, when what is needed is pastoral containment—clear boundaries with continued presence. Disqualification from leadership is not disqualification from love.

Transparency and confidentiality must walk hand in hand. The church must speak the truth, but not in a manner that shames or sensationalizes it. Details should never be shared beyond what is necessary to protect the vulnerable, honor the truth, and initiate restoration. Gossip is not transparency. However, silence that protects injustice is not wisdom, either. The goal is always to preserve trust without destroying dignity.

In especially grievous cases—such as sexual abuse or criminal misconduct—this process also involves cooperating with legal authorities. The stain of sexual abuse is one that the Church has often mishandled, minimizing damage to reputation while maximizing harm to the victim. This must never happen again.

We must unequivocally side with the survivor. This includes removing the accused from leadership, offering trauma-informed care to the victim, and reporting the matter to the appropriate legal agencies. Protection of the vulnerable is a non-negotiable.

However, within the scope of the law and under the wisdom of godly counsel, the Church may still be able to minister to the accused. Restoration does not mean returning to a platform, position, influence, or even public visibility. It may mean never returning to a leadership role. Nevertheless, it can still mean redemption. There is no one who falls outside the reach of God's grace.

Ministering to someone who has done great harm is perhaps one of the most difficult tasks a church can face. It requires enormous wisdom, external help, and a posture of humility and accountability. It demands space for both justice and mercy, for protection and pastoral care, for consequences and compassion.

It may include referrals to counseling centers or specialized ministries. It may involve supervised re-entry into community under pastoral guidance. At no point should the accused be abandoned. Their soul matters too.

If the Church is to be a hospital for sinners, we must be able to treat even the gravely wounded and dangerously sick—with proper quarantine, trained physicians, and care plans that protect the vulnerable and still extend hope to the fallen.

This is how grace responds in the wake of failure—not with panic or public theater, but with presence, courage, and deep pastoral wisdom.

What to Watch For: When Care Becomes a Cover-Up

Sometimes what looks like "care" is actually fear in disguise. Churches may withhold truth, suppress questions, or remove someone quietly, not to preserve dignity, but to protect their own reputation. If the process centers institutional image over individual healing, it risks becoming a spiritual cover-up. True care walks in both truth and love, even when it is uncomfortable.

Practical Markers of Care Before Control

When churches handle failure redemptively, they tend to:
- Prioritize the well-being of all individuals over protecting institutional image.
- Offer immediate pastoral presence rather than public messaging strategies.
- Establish appropriate boundaries without relational exile—even for those not in leadership.
- Balance confidentiality with transparent purpose, avoiding both gossip and secrecy.
- Respond to abuse or criminal conduct by offering care for survivors and involving authorities.

Approach those who have sinned not with abandonment or fear, but with cautious, compassionate boundaries.

15
Step 3: Listening for the Wound
The Work of Spiritual Assessment and Pastoral Guidance

After the initial care and containment phase, the restoration process must proceed deliberately into assessment and spiritual triage. Just as a physician does not begin surgery without first diagnosing the patient, the church must pause to understand what happened, why it happened, and what kind of healing is needed.

This assessment is not about labeling someone as "good" or "bad." It is about identifying wounds, weaknesses, and contributing factors—spiritual, emotional, relational, and circumstantial. Every moral failure has a story, and wise restoration listens to that story without trying to rewrite it or rush it to a tidy conclusion.

This is where a pastoral care team becomes essential. Whether it is elders, outside counselors, or a combination of both, there must be a group of spiritually mature, trauma-informed, and trustworthy leaders who guide the process.

The goals of this team are not punitive. They are pastoral:
- To walk with the fallen individual through self-examination and repentance.

- To uncover patterns of sin, vulnerability, or deception.
- To assess readiness and willingness to engage in healing.
- To ensure the care of others involved is not neglected or overshadowed.
- To discern what kind of restoration is possible, and what kind of boundaries must remain.

This is not a quick interview. It is a journey of deep listening. Often, this phase reveals not just the presenting failure (e.g., an affair, addiction, or abusive behavior) but the deeper fractures underneath—pride, isolation, burnout, fear, or unresolved trauma. These roots must be acknowledged before any healthy rebuilding can begin.

It is also during this phase that spiritual direction can be introduced. Trusted mentors or counselors can walk with the individual through Scripture, confession, and spiritual practices—not as a checklist for return, but as nourishment for the soul. The goal is to reconnect the person not with their former role, but with Christ.

Assessment also requires honest conversations about consequences. Some roles may no longer be appropriate. In the case of abusive patterns or disqualifying sins, leadership may be permanently off the table. This should be communicated with clarity and compassion. When someone knows the road ahead—even if it is different than what they hoped—they can walk it with dignity.

Pastoral guidance also serves to set the tone for the community. A leader or member who shows sincere repentance can be publicly honored, not shamed. A church that sees its shepherds walking people through hard seasons, not just celebrating their victories, becomes a place where healing is normalized.

This is not about creating perfect restoration policies. It is about practicing spiritual wisdom. Every situation is different. Nevertheless, the heart behind assessment should always be: we are here for your soul.

It is here, between exposure and reentry, that the most important work is done. When assessment is thoughtful and pastoral, restoration becomes not only possible but also transformative.

The deeper we are willing to listen, the more powerfully grace can heal.

One danger in assessment is listening with an agenda. If the care team is more focused on labeling the issue or fixing the problem than truly hearing the person, they may miss the deeper wounds entirely. Listening for the wound requires restraint, patience, and a willingness to sit with unresolved pain, rather than seeking tidy conclusions.

Practical Markers of Pastoral Assessment

A healthy spiritual assessment will often include:
- Conversations that uncover both the action and the underlying pain.
- Safe, trusted guides, not interrogators, asking open-ended questions.
- Reflection that leads to deeper self-awareness and repentance.
- Clear, compassionate explanation of possible boundaries and consequences.
- A tone of presence, not pressure; grace, not performance.

16
Step 4: Healing from the Inside Out
Personal Healing and Spiritual Renewal

Once the immediate needs are stabilized and the individual is surrounded with relational support, the process of deeper healing begins. This is not a stage that can be rushed.

Restoration must begin within before any thought of public reintegration can occur.

The danger here is twofold: moving too quickly to "fix" someone through visible restoration, or allowing them to drift in emotional and spiritual limbo with no real direction. What is needed is intentional healing—structured, supportive, and grace-filled. That is where a Personal Healing Plan (PHP) becomes essential.

What Is a Personal Healing Plan?

A Personal Healing Plan is not a list of hoops to jump through. It is a collaborative, pastoral roadmap designed to help the individual who has fallen process their failure, pursue restoration, and return to emotional, spiritual, and relational health. It provides structure without shame, direction without legalism.

The plan should be developed with the guidance of a care team, ideally including:
- A pastoral leader or elder
- A licensed counselor or spiritual director
- A trusted lay mentor or accountability partner

The fallen individual must play an active role in shaping the plan. This is key—it is not something done to them, but something built with them.

Components of the Plan

A strong Personal Healing Plan addresses five interconnected areas of renewal:

Emotional Health — This area acknowledges the inner wounds that contributed to the fall. Healing begins with sessions alongside a professional counselor to process past trauma, grief, or identity wounds. Emotional coping tools must be rebuilt, and regular check-ins with a trusted mentor can help sustain emotional clarity and growth.

Spiritual Renewal — This is not about religious performance, but relational reconnection with God. The plan should help the individual reflect on Scripture rather than just read it, develop a richer prayer life that includes lament and silence, and reenter worship with honesty. A spiritual mentor can walk with them through this process.

Relational Restoration — When trust is broken, it must be rebuilt intentionally. Those who have been harmed should be identified and, when appropriate, invited into restorative conversations. Confession and repentance must be sincere, with boundaries clarified or reestablished. Relationship counseling, especially in family or marital contexts, may also be essential.

Lifestyle and Physical Health — The body and spirit are deeply connected. Restoration involves a reordering of daily life, including healthy sleep, diet, movement, and rest.

The individual may need to step away from draining environments, examine how lifestyle contributed to secrecy or burnout, and remove access to old triggers.

Community Support — True healing cannot happen in isolation. The individual should remain connected to the local church, not as a leader, but as a beloved member. They need space to be vulnerable in a safe setting, such as a small group or a recovery circle. A few trusted people—a "care circle"—should stay close for support, prayer, and accountability.

The Personal Healing Plan is not a rigid contract, but it benefits from milestone reviews:

- 30-day check-in
- 90-day reflection
- 6-month spiritual direction review

The goal is not to "graduate" from brokenness but to measure growth in honesty and health. True healing takes time—often a year or more. Willingness, not perfection, is the key posture. Those who engage in the process must be met with consistency, kindness, and clarity.

A Personal Healing Plan should never become a means to perform or prove worth. If the process becomes about compliance rather than connection, the person may hide their real struggles just to "move forward." True healing happens when the soul is met with grace, not graded by progress.

Why It Matters

The Church often does not know what to do after confession. We either punish or placate. But healing is not automatic, and restoration is not instant. A Personal Healing Plan offers something deeper: a pathway. It says, "We believe God is not finished with you—and we will walk with you until you believe it too."

Practical Markers of True Healing

Signs that the healing process is taking root:
- The individual expresses growing self-awareness, not just regret.
- Emotional resilience increases, and defensive reactions decrease.
- There is consistency in healthy rhythms—spiritually, relationally, and physically.
- The person becomes more open to community, feedback, and healthy boundaries.

17
Step 5: Accountability That Restores
Accountability with Dignity

Accountability is essential to restoration, but it must be the kind that heals, not harms. Too often, churches conflate accountability with surveillance, equating transformation with strict control and constant monitoring. However, biblical accountability is not about policing behavior; it is about walking with someone in truth and love, with the goal of restoration, not restriction.

Accountability is not surveillance. It is not a weekly check-in designed to catch someone doing wrong. It is a shared commitment to help a person become who they are in Christ. That means affirming their worth even as we help them address their weaknesses. Accountability that honors dignity speaks truth without tearing down, offers correction without contempt, and sets boundaries without dehumanization.

A restored person should not be treated like a ticking time bomb, watched with suspicion, or continually reminded of their failure. While there may be guardrails, especially early in the process, those boundaries should feel like scaffolding, not shackles. The point is to support growth, not control the person.

Accountability that Restores

Progress should be measured, not micromanaged. This requires spiritual discernment. There may be milestones, such as a plan to pursue and complete therapy, regular meetings with mentors, and commitments to transparency. However, these should be designed in dialogue with the individual, rather than imposed as a punishment. Ownership increases when the person participates in shaping their healing journey.

Confidentiality is also critical. True accountability requires vulnerability, and vulnerability cannot thrive without trust. Restoration teams must guard what is shared. Information should only be disclosed on a need-to-know basis, and gossip must be treated as a serious breach of the process. If the person feels they are under constant scrutiny from the wider church, they may retreat into silence or shame.

Honest dialogue is the heart of dignified accountability. Check-ins should not feel like performance reviews. They should feel like spiritual conversations. Ask questions that get beneath the surface:

What are you learning about yourself?
Where do you feel God's presence—or His absence?
What has been hardest this week?
Where do you need grace?

Accountability is not about behavior management. It is about identity formation. It is about helping someone remember who they are and whose they are. A fallen believer does not need handlers; they need shepherds, encouragers, truth-tellers, and friends.

When accountability honors dignity, it becomes an instrument of freedom. It does not just keep someone from falling again—it helps them walk taller, eyes lifted, heart open, soul healing.

When accountability becomes about oversight rather than support, it erodes trust. If check-ins feel like inspections instead of invitations, the process risks becoming legalistic. True accountability listens before it corrects, and restores more than it reports.

Practical Markers of Restorative Accountability

- Trust and honesty increase over time, not fear or hiding.
- Feedback flows in both directions, not just top-down.
- Check-ins focus on formation, not failure.
- Boundaries are respected and reviewed, not permanent punishments.

18

Step 6: Restoration with Wisdom
When Grace Sends Again

Restoration ends not with silence but with celebration. If the person has repented, healed, and grown, they can be recommissioned. This may not always mean returning to the same role. It might mean a new role, shaped by new wisdom. What matters most is that grace finishes what it started.

Boundaries vs. Banishment

One of the greatest tensions in restoration is knowing the difference between healthy boundaries and harmful banishment. Setting boundaries is biblical—it protects both the fallen and the flock. On the other hand, banishment cloaked as boundaries causes spiritual trauma.

Jesus practiced boundaries often. He withdrew to pray. He silenced demons. He set conditions for following Him. Let us remember that He never used boundaries to isolate repentant people— He used them to create clarity, space for healing, and a path back to wholeness.

Churches must ask: Are our boundaries designed to restore or to exclude? Are they shaped by fear or by faith? Do they open the door to redemption or reinforce shame?

Here are some markers to help distinguish between boundaries and banishment:

Boundaries are explained; banishment is unexplained.

Boundaries invite participation at a healthy level; banishment removes all access.

Boundaries are reviewed over time; banishment is indefinite and vague.

Boundaries lead to restoration; banishment leads to erasure.

Healthy restoration processes include boundaries, but they reject banishment. They say, "We see your sin, but we also see your story. Let us walk this road of grace together."

Covenant, Not Contract

In some cases, it may be helpful to create a written covenant of accountability with the restored individual. This is not a legal document or disciplinary formality; it is a shared agreement that outlines healthy boundaries, mutual commitments, and ongoing expectations.

Such a covenant affirms grace while clarifying that future failures, especially if patterns repeat, may be addressed differently. It protects both the individual and the church from confusion or inconsistency, ensuring that care remains intentional and transparent.

Tone is everything: this should be a collaborative, prayerful agreement built in trust, not control. Grace welcomes people back, but it also walks with wisdom.

Walking Through Restoration

Restoration is not the final checkpoint; it is a new beginning. Even after someone is restored to a role or welcomed back into the community, they need ongoing support. This includes periodic pastoral check-ins, access to mentorship, and space to share new challenges. The goal is not to monitor, but to accompany.

Restoration is often where new wounds surface: insecurity, fear of judgment, or pressure to perform. That is why churches must build long-term relational scaffolding—not just for restoration, but for resilience. Grace does not just welcome people back—it walks with them forward.

Reinstating Without Reflection

Sometimes, churches eager to move on rush someone back into leadership or visibility without allowing time for true discernment. Reinstating must flow from restoration, not image repair. Wisdom remembers that calling can remain, even when roles change.

Practical Markers of Healthy Restoration

- The individual demonstrates humility, self-awareness, and growth, not just outward compliance.
- Their presence in the community reflects trust-building, not pressure to perform.
- Roles or services emerge naturally and gradually, not through entitlement or demand.
- There is a clear, grace-based support system in place that invites continued connection, not conditional acceptance.

Celebrating Redemption with Grace

When someone returns from a season of brokenness and healing, the church has a holy opportunity—not just to welcome, but to rejoice. Celebration does not mean hype, applause, or platforming. It means naming God's redemptive work with gratitude and humility.

A quiet testimony, a shared prayer, or a communal moment of worship can become sacred acts of acknowledgment: "God restores. Grace is real. Healing is possible."

Celebration reminds the church that no failure is final—and that every return is cause for joy.

19
Collateral Damage and Secondary Wounds
Caring for Those Caught in the Fallout

> *"When elephants fight, it is the grass that suffers."*
> — *African Proverb*

When someone fails, we rightly focus on restoration. However, what about the people left behind in the wreckage? This chapter is for them—the ones whose lives were shaken by proximity, whose wounds are quieter but no less real.

Every failure leaves behind more than one wounded heart. The spouse. The children. The close friend. The loyal ministry teammate. These people often suffer in silence, caught between grief, confusion, and a fear of saying the wrong thing. While the church tends to focus on the individual who failed or caused a public scandal, the emotional wreckage left in the wake is often ignored.

The Overlooked Pain

Spouses are left with unanswered questions and the emotional fallout of betrayal—both from their spouse and, often, from the church. In cases of moral or sexual failure, the pain can be especially raw. The one person they trusted most has fractured that trust, and the church may inadvertently deepen the wound by minimizing their grief, assuming reconciliation is immediate, or focusing entirely on the individual who failed.

When the Children Are Watching

Children may feel anger, shame, confusion, or misplaced blame. They may not understand the failure, but they sense the upheaval. Sudden changes in church involvement, strained relationships at home, or whispered conversations can leave them unsettled and disoriented. Their wounds may not surface immediately. Some children publicly withdraw or act out, while others internalize their pain in silence.

These emotional and spiritual wounds can extend far into adulthood, especially when their questions go unanswered or their pain goes unrecognized. Many lose trust not only in their parent, but in the church itself. If the church avoids them or assumes they are resilient, it deepens their disorientation. Age-appropriate pastoral care, space to ask questions, and reassurance of their belonging are vital.

When Ministry Partners Feel Abandoned

Ministry partners—fellow pastors, leaders, or volunteers—often bear unseen weight. They may feel betrayed by the person who failed, abandoned by leadership, or blamed by the community. Some quietly leave, others stay, but with diminished trust. They need room to grieve what was lost and permission to rebuild without fear of scrutiny. Many also wonder whether their own ministry or reputation is now tainted by association. If the one who failed was their leader or a close collaborator, they may question their discernment, credibility, or future opportunities. This internal questioning—left unspoken—can undermine confidence and call for years to come. Honest conversations, debriefing spaces, and shared lament go a long way in healing fractured ministry teams.

When Friends Are Left in the Middle

Close friends often live in a state of emotional tension. They may feel guilty for not noticing warning signs or confused about how to relate to the one who failed. If they remain loyal, they may be misunderstood. If they distance themselves, they may feel judged. These friends need a compassionate space to process their loss and explore their identity. They must be reminded that friendship does not require pretending and that grief is not betrayal.

Some friends try to stay connected to both the church and the person who has failed, often feeling pulled in opposite directions. They carry relational strain that is rarely acknowledged. These friends must be given a place to voice their concerns without being viewed as disloyal. A healing church affirms its attempt to hold space for both grace and grief—and commits to walking with them, not pressuring them to choose sides.

The Risk of Silence

When the church fails to acknowledge the pain experienced by the family and friends of someone who has fallen short, it unintentionally reinforces isolation. Spouses may feel ashamed to speak. Children may sense they need to protect their parent's image. Friends may withdraw rather than risk saying something wrong. Silence becomes a second wound—often deeper than the first.

The church must normalize care for these secondary wounds, rather than treating them as distractions from the primary restoration. They are not footnotes in someone else's story— they are writing their own chapter of hurt and healing. They, too, need to know that grace sees them.

The Risk of Church Division

In some cases, the individual who fails—whether a beloved pastor, worship leader, long-standing member, or well-connected figure—holds significant emotional weight within the community. When such a person fails, the pain does not just radiate through their close relationships; it fractures the wider church body.

Some grieve quietly. Others defend. Still others leave. Division arises not only from disagreement over what happened, but from how it is handled: too harsh, too soft, too fast, too secretive. Failure can expose fault lines of trust and unity that were already present but unspoken.

The risk of church-wide rupture is real. Furthermore, ignoring it only deepens the divide. A restoring church must be proactive in creating spaces for honest, structured, and grace-filled conversations—not just about what happened, but about what the community needs to process, grieve, and rebuild.

Leaders should expect tension. They should resist defensiveness. Moreover, they should name the pain openly, not defensively. A church that navigates division with humility and transparency has the chance not only to heal but also to become more unified than before.

A Whole-Church Response

Supporting the collateral circle requires intentionality. A few starting points:
- Assign a separate care team or mentor for the spouse or family, not connected to the individual who failed.
- Hold grief and processing groups for ministry peers who have been affected by the failure.

- Invite children or teens into age-appropriate pastoral conversations.
- Regularly check in, even months later, when the public focus has faded.

Restoration becomes a testimony to the church's health not only when the individual is healed, but when those around them feel seen, safe, and supported. That is how a church becomes not just a place of grace, but a people of compassion.

20
When the Fallen Refuse Help

Not everyone who falls is ready—or willing—to be restored. Despite every effort to create a safe, grace-saturated path back into healing, some individuals refuse accountability, reject correction, or deny their failure altogether. When that happens, the church must respond with clarity and compassion, not by escalating shame or washing its hands of the person, but by setting firm boundaries that preserve the health of the body and keep the door of grace open.

Restoration cannot be forced. It is an invitation, not an ultimatum. For it to be genuine, the individual must respond with humility and a desire to grow. If that is absent—if the person becomes combative, manipulative, or completely disengaged—then the restoration process must pause. Continuing to invest energy into someone who has made it clear they are not interested can lead to deeper hurt, both for the community and for the one in need of help.

Churches must take care not to mistake grace for passivity. One danger is slipping into quiet resignation—saying we have left the door open, but in truth, walking away emotionally. If we avoid follow-up entirely or disengage under the guise of being non-coercive, we are not acting in grace—we are avoiding discomfort. Grace does not force, but it also does not forget. It holds space with prayerful expectancy, not silent detachment.

Boundaries protect, but they do not punish. If a fallen leader or member refuses help, it may be necessary to limit their public influence or participation in ministry roles. This is not an act of rejection; it is a stewardship of trust. The community must be protected from spiritual confusion, potential harm, or false reconciliation. These boundaries should be clearly communicated and applied with consistency, not as a consequence for noncompliance, but as a necessary safeguard until healing is pursued.

The Door Remains Open

Even when someone walks away, the church must leave a light on. Like the father in the story of the prodigal son, we do not chase with ultimatums—but we wait with hope. We continue to pray. We refrain from gossip. We speak of them with the belief that grace is still possible. In this, we reflect the nature of God, who never forces repentance, but always welcomes it.

What About Public Perception?

One of the challenges of someone refusing restoration, especially if they are well-known, is that it can create confusion or division in the congregation. In such cases, church leadership should offer a transparent but grace-filled explanation to the community:

"We have extended an opportunity for restoration and healing. At this time, the individual has chosen not to participate. We will honor their decision while continuing to protect our community and remain open to reconciliation, should they seek it."

Grief Is Appropriate

When someone refuses restoration, the church does not just move on. We grieve. We lament. We mourn the broken relationship, the lost opportunities for healing, and the ongoing pain. However, we do not give in to bitterness. We keep our hearts soft. We continue to pray for the story to turn out well.

21
The Church as a Restoring Community

The ministry of restoration is not for the faint of heart. It demands courage, wisdom, humility, and deep love. Nevertheless, it is one of the clearest signs that a church is living in step with the Spirit. When we choose restoration over removal, we embody the gospel. We reflect the Shepherd who leaves the ninety-nine to find the one. We declare that no failure is final and no person is beyond the reach of grace.

May we build churches where stories of restoration are the norm, not the exception. Where fallen leaders are not discarded, but discipled. Where confession is safe. Where trust is rebuilt. Where the broken are not labeled liabilities but welcomed as beloved family.

Imagine a church where the wounded do not hide but come forward knowing they will be met with truth and tenderness, where people are not remembered for their worst moment but for the redemptive journey that followed, where discipline is redemptive, not reactionary. Where tears are not a threat to image, but a testimony to grace.

Such a church becomes more than a gathering—it becomes a healing ground. A community where honesty is not punished but pursued. Where the longer someone stays, the more whole they become.

Restoration is slow work. However, it is holy work. It is the work of the Church—and the legacy of those who dare to lead with grace.

22
Pastoring with Scars

In a church culture obsessed with strength and image, many pastors have been trained to hide their wounds. While this chapter speaks directly to pastors, its themes apply broadly to elders, mentors, ministry leaders, and anyone entrusted with spiritual influence. These principles are for all who shepherd others, regardless of title. But real leadership is not defined by spotless performance, it is shaped in the quiet, gritty places of grace. This chapter is about reclaiming that truth.

The Myth of the Perfect Pastor

For generations, the image of a pastor has been shaped by cultural expectations and institutional pressure. The perfect pastor, we were told, is always composed. Always righteous. Always strong. His marriage is perfect, his children obedient, his sermons eloquent, and his clothes wrinkle-free. He leads with certainty, counsels with wisdom, never doubts, and never fails.

However, that pastor does not exist.

The myth of perfection in ministry has created untold damage. It has led pastors to live double lives—one public and polished, the other private and painful. It has driven men and women to burnout, isolation, and in many tragic cases, moral collapse. When failure finally comes to light, it is not just the action that shocks people, it is the illusion that has been shattered.

No one can live up to the myth. Nor should they try.

Ministry is not about projecting strength. It is about embodying grace. The calling to shepherd others does not require the absence of weakness—it requires the presence of humility.

Put Away the Cape, Put on the Sackcloth

It is time to take off the superhero cape. The Church does not need more celebrity pastors— it needs shepherds. Not polished icons, but broken, honest, Spirit-dependent men and women who are not afraid to say, "I struggle too."

To pastor with scars is not to put wounds on display—it is to stop hiding them. Throughout Scripture, the leaders most used by God were often the most marked by both power and pain. David, called a man after God's own heart, lived a story of anointed leadership shadowed by deep failure. Peter denied Christ in His darkest hour yet became the rock on which the Church was built. Paul, the apostle of grace, openly called himself the "chief of sinners." None of these men led from perfection. They led from redemption.

In ancient Israel, sackcloth was worn during mourning and repentance—a public sign of humility. Perhaps modern pastors need to recover that practice—not literally, but spiritually. To lead from repentance, not performance. To step into the pulpit with a limp, not a mask.

When a pastor takes off the cape and puts on sackcloth, everything changes. It invites others to believe that their struggles do not disqualify them from being worthy. That grace is not just for the strong who keep it together, but for the weary, the flawed, the healing. It tells the truth: that God's power is made perfect in weakness.

Imagine a church where the leader does not pretend to be the hero but always points to Jesus as the only one who truly is—a church where scars are not covered in shame, but honored as reminders of grace. Where strength is found not in control, but in compassion, that is the kind of leadership that draws people in—not because it dazzles, but because it dares to be real.

This is not about glorifying brokenness, it is about dignifying authenticity. Pastors who admit their doubts and wounds do not weaken their authority; they humanize it. They embody the gospel they preach, showing that grace is not just a concept; it is a lifeline.

Sackcloth, after all, has always symbolized humility and repentance. Leaders who choose sackcloth embrace their need for grace and stand in solidarity with the brokenness of their people. They preach not from a platform of perfection, but from a place of transformation.

Putting away the cape means rejecting the illusion that pastors must be invulnerable. The pressure to "have it all together" is more than unhealthy—it is unholy. Leaders who constantly hide behind strength often do so at the cost of their own souls. Ministry becomes a role to play instead of a life to share. Vulnerability is stifled, and eventually, the mask begins to crack.

I have come to believe this: I would rather hear a sinner's description of God than many pastors' description of sin. Why? Because the one who has been forgiven much speaks of grace with a depth that doctrine alone cannot reach. They know what mercy feels like, not just what it is supposed to mean.

Authenticity in leadership does not erode authority—it anchors it. A pastor who admits their need for grace permits everyone else to do the same.

What Qualifies a Leader: Character, Not Image

For too long, churches have elevated charisma over character. We have chosen charm over consistency. We have mistaken giftedness for godliness, and the result has been catastrophic. Time and again, leaders who dazzled from the stage have crumbled in private, leaving behind disillusioned congregations, fractured communities, and wounded faith.

We have built platforms faster than we have built people. We have hired for polish and presence rather than tested for humility, patience, and resilience. But when we elevate image above integrity, we create a culture where appearance matters more than substance, and where failure, when it inevitably comes, is met with either scandal or silence, rather than shepherding.

Scripture is unambiguous about what qualifies someone for leadership. In 1 Timothy 3 and Titus 1, Paul outlines a vision for spiritual leadership that is rooted not in performance but in proven character. Elders and overseers, he writes, must be "above reproach," "not given to drunkenness," "gentle," "not quarrelsome," "faithful to their spouse," "hospitable," and "able to teach." These qualifications are deeply relational and moral. They describe someone who leads their family well, speaks truth without harshness, shows hospitality, and lives with integrity both in public and private.

Paul does not say a leader must be magnetic, eloquent, visionary, or innovative. He says they must be steady, trustworthy, and grounded. Leadership in the Kingdom is not about a platform— it is about a posture. It is about living in a way that reflects the heart of the Shepherd.

That does not mean skills do not matter. Preaching, administration, counseling, and vision casting—these are vital parts of ministry. But skill without soul becomes dangerous. It leads to manipulation instead of ministry, burnout instead of blessing, and spectators instead of disciples.

We do not need more celebrities in pulpits—we need more shepherds in the trenches. We need leaders who know what it is like to walk through grief, to face temptation, to sit in silence with someone who is hurting. Leaders who can say, "I have been there. I am still growing. Let us walk this together."

One of the quiet tragedies of our current church culture is that we often replace fallen leaders not with wiser ones, but with flashier ones. We double down on performance, thinking if we just "wow" people enough, they will forget the pain. However, the truth is, people are not hungry for spectacle; they are hungry for authenticity.

A healthy church must redefine what success in ministry looks like. The question must shift from "How many people showed up?" to "How many people felt seen and shepherded?"

From "How powerful was the sermon?" to "How present was the pastor?" From "How good was the music?" to "How real was the community?"

When we build ministries around charisma, we train people to consume. However, when we build them around character, we train people to become. Moreover, that is the heart of discipleship.

The goal is not to impress. The goal is to be faithful. To be formed into the likeness of Christ. To live in a way where who you are offstage speaks louder than what you do onstage.

In the end, the most powerful testimony of a pastor's life will not be the size of their church— it will be the depth of their love. It will be the quiet stories told in hospital rooms, in living rooms, in late-night prayers for the hurting. It will be the faithfulness that nobody tweets about.

Jesus was not a celebrity. He was a servant. And He is still looking for leaders who are willing to be the same.

Pastors in Recovery: Redemption Stories

If anyone demonstrates the ministry of pastoring with scars, it is Peter. He denied Jesus three times—publicly, fearfully, and with bitter regret. However, Jesus not only restored him but commissioned him: "Feed my sheep." The man who failed spectacularly became the first great leader of the early Church.

Another powerful example is Charles Colson. Once a key figure in the Watergate scandal and labeled Nixon's "hatchet man," Colson served prison time and emerged a transformed man. He founded Prison Fellowship, one of the most significant prison ministry organizations in the world, and became a powerful voice for justice and grace. His leadership flowed directly out of his failure—and his encounter with Christ in the midst of it.

Gordon MacDonald, a respected pastor and author, admitted to moral failure in the late 1980s. He stepped down from ministry and entered a season of intentional restoration, including counseling, accountability, and repentance. Eventually, he returned to leadership with a deepened humility and wisdom that shaped his writing and mentoring for decades to come.

These stories remind us that failure is not final when grace is involved. The power of redemption lies not in excusing sin, but in allowing God to bring healing and purpose from brokenness. Pastors who have failed but choose the hard road of repentance and restoration offer the Church something far more powerful than a polished image—they offer hope.

They teach us that no one is too far gone. That grace is not theoretical. Moreover, that leadership forged in the fire of failure can become the most trustworthy kind.

The Church needs pastors with scars—not because scars are glamorous, but because they are real. They prove we have wrestled and that we have limped, moreover, that we have lived to testify not to our strength, but to His.

Let the Church be led by those who have tasted grace—and are not afraid to pass the cup to others.

23
Structures That Serve the Spirit

> *"Where the Spirit of the Lord is, there is freedom."*
> — *2 Corinthians 3:17*

Church governance might seem like the least spiritual topic in the world, but how we lead shapes what we become. If our systems reflect fear, control, or secrecy, we disciple people into dysfunction. However, if our structures reflect grace, transparency, and trust, we create space for the Spirit to flourish. This chapter is not just about policy—it is about people.

When church governance structures fail to reflect the heart of Christ, they not only hinder growth but also harm people. Too often, well-meaning systems become spiritual bottlenecks. Policies are wielded as power plays. Boards become more concerned with image management than soul care. In the name of order, we lose the organic, life-giving work of the Spirit.

However, church structures do not have to work against grace. When aligned with the Spirit, they can serve as trellises—supporting healthy growth, providing accountability without abuse, and fostering environments where trust can flourish. This chapter explores what it means to rebuild church systems that serve the Spirit rather than sabotage it.

Accountability That Is not Adversarial

Churches need accountability, but accountability does not have to be synonymous with suspicion or surveillance. In healthy systems, accountability is about alignment with mission and mutual submission. It is not about control—it is about care.

Too often, accountability is reactive, triggered only when a problem arises. Instead, it should be proactive, woven into the rhythms of leadership life. A pastor or leader with no one to answer to is a spiritual hazard waiting to happen. However, a pastor who lives in mutual accountability with peers, elders, mentors, and even congregants is more likely to grow in humility, rather than hubris.

In adversarial models, accountability takes the form of interrogation: "What did you do wrong?" In grace-shaped systems, it takes the form of inquiry: "How are you really doing?"

Churches can develop non-adversarial accountability through:

- Regular spiritual check-ins among leaders, focused on heart health, not just performance.
- Peer mentoring—not just reporting to a board but walking with someone who knows your story.
- Spaces for mutual confession and prayer, where leaders model the vulnerability they ask of others.

How would it look if your church began asking one simple question at every leadership meeting: "Where have you needed grace this month?" At first, the answers might be guarded. However, over time, a culture of vulnerability could emerge—not as a sign of weakness, but as a source of spiritual strength. When leaders share about burnout, doubt, or spiritual dryness, it invites prayer, not shame. It models trust instead of fear, and it signals to the whole community that honesty is safe and grace is available.

Governing, Bylaws, and Broken Trust

Many of the breakdowns in trust that plague churches are not caused by bad theology but by broken systems. Governing boards, whether referred to as elder boards, leadership teams, or church councils, that are disconnected, overly controlling, or unclear in purpose, often do more harm than good. When bylaws are opaque or manipulated to serve a power structure, the Spirit's work is stifled.

We must begin by asking: What is the role of elders? Biblically, elders are shepherds, not CEOs. Their function is to guide, protect, and nurture the flock—not to function as a corporate board fixated on financial oversight or institutional preservation.

However, in many churches, elder boards often become power brokers, becoming more involved in approving budgets and buildings than in pastoring souls. Furthermore, when conflict arises—especially involving staff—the board's default is often to protect the church's reputation rather than seek redemptive resolution.

What happens when a board has no clear bylaws, or worse, does not follow the ones it has? Confusion, inconsistency, and distrust take root. A church without clearly communicated and consistently upheld governance structures becomes vulnerable to the misuse of authority.

The people have no map to follow and no assurance that decisions are being made with integrity. Bylaws that are outdated, inaccessible, or arbitrarily enforced serve no one well, and they erode both spiritual and structural credibility.

To rebuild trust:
- Church boards must reframe their identity around spiritual leadership, regardless of their

specific titles or structure. Their primary job is to shepherd, not manage.
- Bylaws should be transparent and available to the congregation. If the people do not know how decisions are made, they will assume the worst. Churches should regularly review and update their bylaws, incorporating congregational input and maintaining clarity of purpose.
- Term limits, regular evaluations, cross-training in both elder and deacon functions where applicable, and formation in spiritual leadership can ensure elders stay fresh, focused, and faithful.

Churches must also wrestle with the question: Are we structured for control or care? Do our systems serve the people, or do they serve the other way around? Moreover, if your church operates with a single group filling both elder and deacon roles, have they been given tools to discern which hat they are wearing in the moment and how to strike a healthy balance?

Transparent Processes for Discipline and Restoration

One of the most sensitive areas of church governance is how we handle failure, especially among leaders. Unfortunately, most churches only consider restoration processes after a crisis has occurred. This leaves them scrambling to react rather than leading with clarity and care.

When there are no visible pathways for confession and restoration, secrecy becomes the norm. Leaders hide struggles. Staff members suffer in silence. The church becomes a place where honesty feels dangerous.

To counter this, churches must develop and communicate transparent processes for discipline and restoration before they are needed.

These processes should include:

- A clear definition of what constitutes disqualification. Not every mistake is a reason for removal. Not every sin is a scandal.
- A tiered system of response—minor issues handled with mentoring and support; major breaches addressed with formal plans.
- A restoration team or panel, composed of spiritually mature, trusted individuals who walk with the person through confession, counseling, restitution, and reintegration.

Importantly, transparency does not mean airing dirty laundry to the congregation. It means having an agreed-upon protocol, so that when information is shared, it is done with wisdom, consistency, and grace.

An Example of Transparent Discipline

Imagine a situation where a pastor admits to struggling with pornography. In some churches, this confession would immediately lead to removal, shaming, or silence. However, in a grace-formed structure, the process might look different:

- The pastor confesses to a peer or elder.
- A confidential team meets with the pastor, listens, and discerns next steps.
- A temporary leave is initiated—not as punishment, but as space for healing.
- A counselor is assigned. A spiritual mentor is engaged. A personal growth plan is created.
- The congregation is informed with a general, truthful statement: *"Pastor John is taking a leave to address some personal spiritual concerns. He is walking through a care and restoration plan supported by the elders."*

This approach preserves dignity, invites prayer, and models what it means to take sin seriously without turning restoration into a form of punishment.

Structures That Serve Relationships, Not Replace Them

Perhaps the most overlooked reality in church governance is that structure can never replace relationship. No bylaw, job description, or policy will ever substitute for trust. Healthy churches are built on healthy relationships, and structures are simply the scaffolding.

When leaders relate only through structures, they become transactional. When relationships are nurtured in the Spirit, they become transformational.

What this means practically:

- Have more conversations than memos.
- Do not hide behind "the board decided..." Invite people into the process where appropriate.
- Make room for feedback, especially from those without power. Create forums, surveys, and listening sessions to gather feedback.
- Make decisions in prayer, not just in policy. A Spirit-led board does not just vote; it discerns.

Structures That Are Subject to the Winds of the Spirit

One of the hidden dangers in modern church models is over-structuring. Everything is systematized, branded, delegated, and measured. However, when every moment is programmed, we leave little room for the Spirit.

A healthy structure does not mean rigid schedules or authoritarian control. It means clarity that leads to freedom, not restriction.

Ask these questions:

- Do our systems make room for interruption, for prayer, for pause?
- Are our staff meetings moments of ministry—or just logistics?
- Do our worship gatherings follow a script or flow from a shared hunger for God?

Structures should be Spirit-sensitive. That means:
- Sabbath is honored. Busyness is not spiritual.
- Silence is welcomed. The Holy Spirit does not always shout.
- Flexibility is possible. Plans can change if the Spirit is leading.

Governance As a Form of Discipleship

Ultimately, every system in the church teaches something. How we govern teaches our people how to think about power, conflict, grace, and truth. If our systems are marked by secrecy, control, and rigidity, our people will absorb those traits as "normal Christianity."

When our structures reflect the Spirit of Christ—marked by mutual submission, hospitality, transparency, and hope—we disciple our people into a better way.

Governance is not a side issue. It is a discipleship issue, and churches that want to grow in grace must be willing to reform not just their preaching, but their policy.

When Policy Becomes Prayer

Structures can be beautiful servants but brutal masters. The difference lies in who is at the center. When Christ is central and the Spirit is welcomed, even the most mundane processes become holy ground. Board meetings become spaces of prayer. Budget discussions become acts of faith. Discipline becomes a doorway to healing.

May our churches rebuild systems that support the life of the Spirit. That offers stability without suffocation. That protects the flock while empowering the shepherds. May our policies reflect our theology, and our governance be shaped, not by fear or control, but by love.

This is what it means to build structures that serve the Spirit.

24
The Role of the Congregation

The Church as a Body

The congregation is not an audience—it is the living, breathing body of Christ. While leadership may set the tone, it is often the collective life of the members that determines whether a church culture becomes one of healing or harm. Wounds in the church are not only inflicted by the pulpit but also in the pews. Likewise, healing does not only flow from pastors, but also through the hands and hearts of everyday believers.

Scripture is clear: Christ alone is the head of the Church (Ephesians 1:22–23). Nevertheless, many congregations continue to operate under a corporate hierarchy that mistakenly elevates the pastor to the top of an organizational chart, as if the church were a company and the people its consumers. However, the biblical vision of the Church is far more akin to organic chemistry than to an organizational structure—living bonds and interconnected relationships, where each part serves the other, and each member is necessary to the health of the whole.

Paul's metaphor of the Church as a body in 1 Corinthians 12 further illustrates this organic design. "Just as a body, though one, has many parts, but all its many parts form one body, so it is with Christ... Now you are the body of Christ, and each one of you is a part of it" (1 Corinthians 12:12-27). In this vision, no role is insignificant, no gift dispensable. The eye needs the hand; the head cannot say to the feet, "I do not need you."

This is not just poetic language—it is structural theology. The Church is not defined by top-down control, but by mutual dependence. Authority exists, but it functions within the greater call to unity and humility. When the body functions in love, every ligament is strengthened. When it does not, disease spreads quickly.

A Vision for a Living Congregation

Before examining the challenges in a congregation and how to address them, it is worthwhile to consider the possibility of a congregation fully alive in the Spirit. A church where the bonds of fellowship are thick with grace. Where Sunday gatherings are not events to attend but expressions of a shared life. Where prayer requests are not whispered obligations, but doorways to spiritual friendship.

In this kind of congregation, spiritual gifts are not just acknowledged but activated. The teacher teaches. The encourager encourages. The helper serves. The prophet speaks with humility and clarity. Everyone contributes, and everyone is discipled. Worship is not a performance but a chorus of participation. Hospitality flows through every home and hallway. Prayer requests are actually taken up by each other in prayer and not simply fodder for the latest gossip.

This congregation is not perfect, but it is alive. It bleeds when someone hurts. It rejoices when someone returns. It stretches to include the newcomer and honors the legacy of the seasoned saint. It is not obsessed with relevance or performance, but with presence. In this environment, grace is not a slogan—it is the air they breathe.

When the congregation gets it right, it becomes a living demonstration of the gospel. People step into church expecting judgment but find joy. They expect to be ignored, but instead, they are embraced. Hospitality is not just a handshake at the door—it is a community that invites you into its heart. Volunteers serve not out of obligation but from delight. Confession becomes part of the culture—not in hushed tones, but in courageous truth-telling that leads to prayer and healing. A vibrant congregation does not just attend church; they become the Church, and in doing so, they show the world what Jesus looks like.

Let us examine some of the issues that impact its health.

Gossip vs. the Gospel

One of the greatest threats to congregational health is gossip—the unofficial "grapevine" that spreads speculation, half-truths, and condemnation like a virus. Scripture speaks plainly: "A perverse person stirs up conflict, and a gossip separates close friends" (Proverbs 16:28). What begins as curiosity often devolves into character assassination.

When someone fails, especially a leader, the vacuum of information quickly fills with rumors. Rather than wait for the truth, the congregation sometimes jumps to judgment.

Instead of bearing one another's burdens (Galatians 6:2), we broadcast brokenness.

The Gospel community rejects this. It leans in, listens well, and confronts sin without shaming. A healthy congregation refuses to pass along what it has not prayed over. It speaks words that heal rather than harm, and when gossip arises, it responds with grace and clarity: "That is not ours to share."

The Power of Perseverance

In times of church crisis, people tend to scatter. Attendance dips. Giving drops. It is too easy to pick up and just find another church, one where you can simply be entertained and not have to endure the pain. Moreover, those most affected—often the fallen, the hurting, or the accused—find themselves abandoned and vulnerable. However, there is a profound power in not leaving but simply staying with the body.

Faithfulness is a congregational calling. When a member is hurting, showing up matters: a phone call, a visit, a meal dropped off without fanfare. When someone confesses, our reflex should not be to retreat but to embrace.

There are untold stories of congregants who refused to walk away. A couple who sat beside a disgraced elder. A friend who brought communion to someone who was too ashamed to return to church. These small acts become sacraments. They teach the church to hold space for brokenness without withdrawing love.

Practicing Reconciliation in the Pews

Forgiveness is not a top-down command. It is a horizontal practice. Jesus said that before we offer our gifts at the altar, we must be reconciled to our brother or sister (Matthew 5:23– 24). This is not just a leadership ethic—it is a call to every believer.

Congregations must foster a culture where members pursue peace with one another. This means asking for forgiveness when we speak carelessly. It means receiving confrontation with humility. It means refusing to weaponize others' wounds in spiritual conversations. I find it important to point out that we do not need to wait for someone to ask for forgiveness before we forgive them. Remember Christ's words on the cross: "Forgive them, for they know not what they do." Forgiveness is extended as an act of grace, not a response to an apology.

Asking for forgiveness or apologizing is a completely separate act—that is the act of repentance.

Imagine communion not only as a sacred meeting between you and God, but as a sacred opportunity for reconciliation with one another. What if, before taking the elements, the church did not simply bow in silent reflection, but also looked up, scanned the room, and moved toward those with whom they have held offense? Not to grandstand or draw attention, but to say quietly and sincerely, "I forgive you... I am with you... and I am sorry I let that wound linger in my heart."

Communion becomes more than a ritual; it becomes a reunion. A space where fractured relationships begin to heal, where grace moves not just down from heaven, but across the pews. This is how the gospel is not only preached, but embodied—in the courageous love that mends what was broken.

A Posture of Graceful Service

In John 13, Jesus stooped to wash the feet of His disciples—not to create a ritual, but to reveal a posture: humility, presence, and grace. He said, "Now that I, your Lord and Teacher, have washed your feet, you also should wash one another's feet." This was not about hygiene—it was about heart.

While few churches today practice literal foot washing, the spirit of that act remains vital. What does it look like to wash one another's feet today? It looks like listening without defensiveness and forgiving without fanfare and offering presence without performance and holding space for another's sorrow, and doing so without superiority.

To serve like Jesus is to kneel, not to climb. It is to take the low place, not as a show of piety, but as a way of love. A congregation that serves this way does not try to impress— it tries to bless. It remembers that everyone carries dust from the road. Furthermore, everyone— eventually—needs to be met with grace.

When the Church Becomes a Healing Community

While the previous section explored spiritual service, this section steps back to reflect on the bigger picture: what happens when the entire congregation leans into grace. Some churches model this well. In these congregations, transparency is met with trust. Where confession is not a scandal, but sacred ground, in such places, leaders are not left to bear failure alone. The congregation walks with them, not to excuse, but to restore.

The ripple effects are remarkable: marriages are healed, friendships are restored, and younger generations are discipled in grace. People return, not for programs, but for presence. The church becomes known, not for its polish, but for its peace. The community starts to resemble the Kingdom. Outsiders become family. Brokenness becomes testimony, and grace flows without obstruction.

When the congregation lives this out, it becomes the clearest signpost to the world that Jesus is not a relic of the past, but a living presence among His people.

This is what it means to be a healing congregation: not a passive audience, but an active, Spirit-formed body. We are not spectators of grace—we are stewards of it. When we choose love over judgment, presence over withdrawal, reconciliation over gossip, we show the world what Jesus looks like among His people.

25
When Churches Repent

The Power of Collective Repentance

Repentance is often understood as a deeply personal act—an individual turning from sin and returning to God. However, there is a deeper, more comprehensive version of repentance that the modern church often overlooks: collective repentance. This is the repentance of a body, a people, a system that recognizes it has gone astray. It is what happens when a church stops blaming individuals and starts asking, "What have we become?"

Churches, like people, can sin. They sin by what they allow, by what they ignore, by the culture they protect, and the people they harm through silence or secrecy. When leaders cover up abuse, protect reputations, or suppress questions in the name of unity, they participate in a form of corporate rebellion—one that grieves the heart of God just as surely as individual sin does.

Collective repentance begins with this realization: we did not just make a mistake—we built a culture that made it likely. It is not enough to fire the pastor, release a statement, or wait for the news cycle to move on. Those actions may be necessary, but they are not repentance. Repentance involves confession, lament, restitution, and transformation. It is not a press release—it is a posture.

This pattern of collective repentance is deeply rooted in Scripture. Israel, time and again, had to confront not just the sins of individuals but the rebellion of the nation. In the days of Nehemiah, after the walls of Jerusalem were rebuilt, the people gathered together, fasting and wearing sackcloth, confessing "the sins of Israel" and reading from the Law for hours (Nehemiah 9). They did not point fingers at specific wrongdoers—they collectively owned their shared failure.

In Daniel 9, we see Daniel, a righteous man by all accounts, repenting on behalf of his people. "We have sinned and done wrong," he prays, not "they." He identifies with the failures of his nation and intercedes with humility and urgency. Similarly, Ezra tore his garments in grief, fell on his knees, and cried out to God over the unfaithfulness of the people (Ezra 9). These were not merely individual laments. They were a national reckoning, and they were met with mercy.

When churches today embrace the same posture, they step into a biblical legacy of transformation. Churches must rediscover that repentance is not weakness. It is strength, not defeat. It is discipleship. It is the first act of revival.

And when a church repents, when it dares to say publicly, "We were wrong," it opens the door for healing not only for its own members, but for those watching from the outside— those who have been hurt, those who have left, and those who have stopped believing the church could ever be safe again. It invites not just the congregation but the broader community into the process. Let us be clear: it is not only congregations that can discern authenticity—the world can tell too. A hollow apology rings louder than silence.

This is why the Church must move beyond viewing itself as merely a congregation. The early Church in Acts was not a collection of spectators; it was a Spirit-bonded community, a shared life. Acts 2:42–47 describes a people devoted to teaching, fellowship, prayer, and the breaking of bread, holding all things in common. The Church was—and is—a living body, not a stage performance. When one part suffers, all suffer (1 Corinthians 12:26).

Repentance must flow through the whole system.

Public Confession and Congregational Healing

One of the most difficult but redemptive steps a church can take is public confession. It means standing before the community members, former members, and even those outside the walls—and naming what was done wrong. This is not easy, especially in a culture conditioned to defend and deflect. However, confession is the door to healing.

When church leadership openly acknowledges its failures, it models vulnerability, humility, and responsibility. It also communicates to the congregation that truth is more important than image. Whether the issue is spiritual abuse, moral failure, systemic favoritism, or silence in the face of injustice, naming it in public disarms the shame and secrecy that so often plague religious institutions.

Best practices for public confession include careful preparation, clear and concise language, and a commitment to ongoing dialogue. Public statements should be truthful but not defensive, transparent but not reckless. In some cases, it may be helpful to include the voices of those who have been harmed, if they are willing and supported. A church that invites testimony—not just from leaders but from laypeople—starts to rebuild trust.

The impact of a genuine confession is profound. Congregations often respond not with outrage, but with relief. Finally, someone is saying what everyone knew. Finally, the gaslighting stops. This moment of truth-telling can become a moment of deep emotional release—tears, lament, and even hope.

However, confession alone is not enough. Furthermore, if it becomes performative—just another polished event or PR strategy—it loses its redemptive power. Churches must resist the urge to manage optics and instead embrace authenticity. This is not about salvaging reputation; it is about seeking reconciliation. Congregations can tell when confession is scripted versus when it is sincere. So can the world.

True healing requires consistent, courageous actions. Churches should create intentional spaces for processing grief and healing. This might include:

- Town hall meetings where people can ask questions
- Listening sessions with trained facilitators
- Prayer gatherings centered around lament and intercession
- Small group discussions on spiritual abuse and restoration

When done well, public confession becomes a turning point. It is the hinge on which the future swings—not away from the past, but through it, into a more honest and grace-filled church culture.

Leadership Turnover and New Vision

Repentance sometimes requires changes in leadership. While not all failure demands resignation, some failures are too damaging for a leader to remain in place, especially if trust has been broken or abuse has occurred. A clean break may be necessary to protect the vulnerable and make space for healing. However, the goal should never be punishment—it should be restoration, even if that restoration happens outside a leadership role.

However, there are also times when a temporary step down is possible. In cases where a leader is repentant and the failure, while serious, does not involve disqualification (such as criminal or abusive behavior), the church can consider a path to eventual restoration.

This requires careful discernment, outside accountability, and transparent communication with the congregation. An interim pastor from outside the community can offer support and stability during the transition. Likewise, elders or lay leaders can step up to teach and shepherd in the interim.

There are also moments when a leader, though not personally at fault, chooses to step aside to make space for the congregation to grieve, reflect, and heal. This is not abdication, but humble leadership. By relinquishing control, the leader allows fresh voices to rise, helping guide the church through a season of transformative repentance.

This may look like a sabbatical, a step back from preaching, or a temporary shift in role— from leading the charge to quietly walking alongside others. In fact, sabbaticals can also serve as preventative tools—giving leaders regular space for rest, reflection, and recalibration before burnout or crisis emerges. A rhythm of retreat can build a culture of sustainability, not survival. Remaining in the community while relinquishing authority models servant leadership at its best.

A temporary stepping aside allows the leader time for healing, counseling, and reflection. It also signals to the congregation that leadership is not about image maintenance, but spiritual integrity. Importantly, this decision must not be made in a vacuum; it should be developed prayerfully with wise counsel, and the timeline for restoration should be clear and revisited regularly.

In any leadership change, it is vital that the church also cast a new vision—not just about structure, but about heart. A new beginning is not just a reshuffling of roles. It is a re-commitment to Christlike leadership, authentic community, and servant-hearted mission. Congregations that have walked through confession and repentance together are often uniquely positioned to birth something new. Their scars can become their testimony.

Signs of Sincere Institutional Repentance

So, how do we know when a church has truly repented, not just issued a statement, but been transformed?

The signs are not flashy. They are rarely the stuff of social media virality. They are usually slow, steady, and deeply spiritual. Here are some of the key indicators:

- Culture shifts before programs do. Real repentance changes the environment, not just the events. You sense it in the tone of conversations, the posture of leaders, the way hard questions are welcomed instead of avoided.
- Victims are prioritized, not managed. A repentant church listens to survivors of harm. It believes them. It walks with them without defensiveness. It invites their voices into the healing process, not as tokens, but as partners.
- Power becomes shared, not hoarded. Authority is re-examined. Boards become more transparent. Elders are retrained. New leaders emerge who understand the cost of control and the value of grace.
- Policies are rewritten—not just to prevent harm, but to promote wholeness. From bylaws to hiring practices to how conflict is handled, a repenting church rethinks its structure with spiritual health in mind.
- Worship and lament live together. Songs of joy are no longer disconnected from the stories of pain in the room. There is room in the liturgy for grief. There is space for silence. Communion becomes a table of reconciliation, not performance.
- People come back. Maybe not everyone, and maybe not right away—but slowly, some of those who left begin to return. Not because everything is fixed, but because they see it is being faced. They see a community willing to do the deep, unglamorous work of love.

The ultimate fruit of institutional repentance is not a better brand—it is a more beautiful body. A church that has learned to tell the truth about itself becomes a church where others feel safe to tell the truth about themselves.

As we continue this journey of becoming a healing Church, we must resist the temptation to seek closure over change. Repentance is not a one-time moment. It is an ongoing commitment to truth, humility, and the Spirit-led transformation of our communities.

26
The Power of Lament

Why Lament Matters

In our results-oriented church culture, lament is often misunderstood, neglected, or altogether avoided. Many churches equate spiritual maturity with positivity, framing sorrow as something to be overcome quickly with praise. However, the biblical witness reveals that lament is not the opposite of faith; rather, it is a profound expression of it. In fact, lament is one of the most theologically rich forms of worship in Scripture.

The Psalms are filled with laments—nearly a third of them. The prophets lamented. Jesus Himself lamented over Jerusalem. Paul spoke of groaning in the Spirit. The early Church not only rejoiced; it grieved together. When we lament, we join this sacred tradition.

Lament gives us the language of grief, the rhythm of sorrow, the space to name our losses and ask our hardest questions.

More than personal grief, lament is essential for the corporate body. When a church experiences division, betrayal, moral failure, or the slow attrition of trust and belonging, lament is the soul's necessary response. We cannot heal what we refuse to feel. Lament allows the body to grieve together, not in isolated whispers but in unified humility before God.

Contrary to the modern impulse to "move on," lament slows us down. It refuses the quick fix. It creates space for the Holy Spirit to meet us in our questions, our anger, our ache. It is, in many ways, a holy protest: against injustice, against sin, against the silence that too often suffocates the wounded. Lament says, "This should not be," and in doing so, it honors the heart of God who came to redeem what has been broken.

Lament also gives voice to the MIAs of church life—those who once were among us but are now absent due to pain, betrayal, disillusionment, or burnout. It names the ache we feel when pews are emptier, not because people moved away, but because they were pushed away or quietly slipped out. Lament creates a sacred space to remember them without shame or blame.

Lament is not just free-form sorrow. It follows a shape, often mirroring the steps of grief. These include:

- Acknowledgment – We name the loss, the wrong, the fracture. Lament begins when we stop pretending that everything is fine.
- Protest – We bring our holy frustration before God. Like the psalmists, we cry, "How long, O Lord?" Lament gives voice to the injustice and pain.
- Petition – We ask for help, healing, justice, restoration. Lament is not passive—it pleads with God to act.
- Trust – Most laments end not with resolution, but with surrender. "Yet I will trust in You." Lament strengthens faith not by removing pain but by anchoring us to God in the middle of it.

Lament, then, is not a detour from the spiritual journey. It is a bridge, and it must become part of the collective vocabulary of a church that seeks to heal, reconcile, and grow in grace.

Remembering the Wounded

Communal lament is incomplete if it does not include those who have been wounded by the very community that now seeks healing. This is especially important in churches that are reckoning with their past—be it a moral failure by leadership, a toxic culture, or a history of exclusion.

Often, when churches move forward without acknowledging the pain of those who have left, they deepen the wound. Those who departed are left feeling forgotten, erased, or dismissed. But lament remembers.

Some wounds are too deep for quick words. Lament honors that. It says, "We see you. We miss you. We mourn that you were hurt here." In some cases, churches may even hold a service of remembrance for those who have left, not to shame or coerce return, but to confess and intercede. To say, publicly and prayerfully, that the body is not whole without them.

Just as lament follows the steps of grief—acknowledgment, protest, petition, and trust, as outlined earlier—so too must our remembering follow this path. We acknowledge the reality of harm. We protest the ways we have allowed it. We petition God for healing and reconciliation. Furthermore, we trust that He is near to the brokenhearted (Psalm 34:18).

This remembering is not just about the past. It is a declaration that our future will be different. It is a commitment to no longer silence pain or sweep conflict under the rug. It is a sacred act of hospitality, creating space for the wounded to return, not to a triumphant institution, but to a community humbled by grief and anchored in grace.

The Power of Lament

Communal Sorrow as Holy Ground

When a church enters into lament together, it is not a step backward—it is a sacred advance into maturity. Shared sorrow creates holy ground because it invites the presence of the God who "is close to the brokenhearted and saves those who are crushed in spirit" (Psalm 34:18).

Communal sorrow reminds us that we are not alone in our grief. It knits us together. It breaks down the illusion of self-sufficiency and opens the way for compassion. In shared lament, we begin to shoulder one another's burdens—not with fixes, but with presence.

This holy ground can be messy. Tears may come. Confessions may surface. However, in these moments, we are never closer to the heart of Christ. For He was "a man of sorrows, acquainted with grief" (Isaiah 53:3). He entered our pain, bore our shame, and showed us that even the darkest lament can lead to resurrection.

When visitors enter a church during a season of lament, it is natural to feel uncertain about what to say or how to present ourselves. The answer is not to make excuses or apologize for not offering a polished, upbeat experience. Instead, we can be honest. We can say, "You are visiting us during a sacred season. We are grieving some things together.

You are welcome to join us—not as spectators of a performance, but as fellow humans in need of grace."

That transparency is not off-putting; it is disarming. It may be the most authentic thing a guest has seen in church in years. Services in lament are not less spiritual—they are deeply sacred. They reveal a community's willingness to face hard truths in the presence of a gracious God. They offer something the world rarely does: space to be broken and still belong.

Churches that make space for lament do not lose their power—they discover it. They do not become weak; they become wise. They become known not just for their music, teaching, or programs, but for their tenderness. Their honesty. Their ability to sit in the ashes without rushing to sweep them away.

Lament is not where the church dies. It is often where it begins to live truly.

"Those who sow with tears will reap with songs of joy."
— Psalm 126:5

27
The Sound of Honest Worship

Worship is not just the musical portion of the church service—it is far more. It is the posture of the heart before God. True worship encompasses every part of our lives and liturgy: how we sing, how we confess, how we pray, how we listen, how we gather, and how we respond. Worship is not a warm-up act for the sermon or a spiritual entertainment break. It is the church's communal expression of reverence, joy, sorrow, hope, and surrender. This does not mean excellence is wrong, but when excellence overshadows authenticity, we lose the heart of worship.

Unfortunately, in many churches, worship has become a performance. The lights, the sound, and the production are not evil in themselves, but they can mask a deeper problem. When worship is designed primarily to impress or to generate an emotional high, it can bypass the real, gritty, and necessary engagement with God. It can avoid pain. It can silence honesty. Moreover, most tragically, it can train people to equate God's presence with a mood.

We need worship that tells the truth, and sometimes, the most honest expression of worship is not a song—it is silence.

The Need for Silence

Silence is one of the most neglected elements of worship in the modern church. In a culture of constant noise, where every moment of a service is filled with sound, we have forgotten how to be still before God. We fear silence. It makes us uncomfortable. It leaves space for awkwardness, for uncertainty. However, silence is sacred.

In many prayer meetings, the moment the prayer begins, so does the music. Soft pads, gentle chords, background melodies—designed, perhaps, to help us focus. However, often, they distract. They occupy. They prevent us from hearing the still, small voice of God or from noticing what is rising in our own hearts.

The Quakers—also known as the Religious Society of Friends—have long understood what many churches have forgotten: silence is not absence—it is invitation. In their unprogrammed meetings, the entire service may be spent in shared stillness, unless the Spirit moves someone to speak. This kind of silence is not empty, but expectant. It levels all voices, builds community, and allows space for deep inner searching.

We have much to learn from that tradition. Silence allows room for lament. It creates a holy space for individuals to process grief, conviction, or praise in their own way. It reminds us that worship is not just a private moment with God, but a communal act—one where we can hear each other's groans, feel each other's presence, and share a space that is not filled with the dominance of any single voice.

Being uncomfortable in silence is okay. In fact, it may be the most spiritual moment of the service. Discomfort moves us—it reveals what we hide, what we fear, what we long for. It invites us to lean into God's presence with vulnerability, rather than rely on the structure of familiar noise.

The Sound of Honest Worship

Imagine a church service where, after a song or prayer, the room is allowed to be silent for two or three full minutes. Imagine what could surface in that quiet: a whispered confession, a tear, a simple "thank you," a stirring to kneel or lift one's hands. Silence is not the absence of worship—it is a form of it.

Worship That Includes Confession

The early church incorporated confession as a normal part of its worship rhythm, not as an admission of defeat, but as a recognition of God's mercy. Confession is not the opposite of praise—it is a doorway into it. When we confess, we declare the truth about ourselves and the truth about God: that we are broken, and He is gracious.

Corporate worship that includes confession allows the whole church to practice humility together. It breaks the illusion that some have "arrived" while others are barely hanging on. It levels the room.

Simple practices—such as a shared prayer of confession, time for silent reflection, or opportunities for reconciliation—can transform a worship gathering. They remind us that we are not here to impress God or each other. We are here to be changed.

Songs for the Struggler, the Saint, and the Furnace

Our worship playlists must reflect the full emotional range of the human experience. The Psalms teach us this. They include hymns of celebration, cries of desperation, declarations of trust, and groans of pain.

If we only sing songs of triumph, we alienate those who are mourning. If we only focus on victory, we abandon those in the middle of a battle. A healthy worship culture includes space for minor chords. For tears. For "How long, O Lord?"

Many of the church's most beloved hymns and worship songs were not written from mountaintops of spiritual ecstasy, but from valleys of suffering. "It Is Well with My

Soul" was penned by Horatio Spafford after the death of his four daughters at sea. "Come Thou Fount of Every Blessing" was written by Robert Robinson, who would later wrestle with deep spiritual drifting. Even the contemporary worship movement includes songs like Matt Redman's "Blessed Be Your Name", written in response to personal and national tragedy.

These songs endure because they speak truth to the whole of life. They remind us that worship is not about how we feel—it is about who God is. When we sing these words, forged in the fire of grief and trial, we do not just remember their stories—we enter into a shared witness of faith that clings to God in all seasons.

When we sing songs that tell the truth, we build a church that can withstand the storms. We disciple people not just to shout in joy, but to cry out in pain, and in doing so, we echo the faith of Christ Himself, who sang a psalm of lament as He hung on the cross.

The Heart of Worship

Worship that tells the truth does not perform—it testifies. It becomes a sacred act of communal honesty, forming us not around a genre or a sound, but around the God who meets us in both triumph and trial.

In rethinking our worship practices, let us resist the pressure to perform and instead return to the heart of worship: Christ at the center, truth in our songs, silence in our space, and grace on our lips.

May our churches become places where silence is welcome, confession is freeing, and every voice finds its place in the song—not because we all sound the same, but because we worship the One who hears us all.

28
The Church with Open Arms

For too long, the Church has subtly taught that grace is gated. Belonging must be earned. You must first clean up before you can come in. This stands in stark contrast to the life and ministry of Jesus.

Jesus' Inclusive Ministry and the Call to Emulate It

Jesus welcomed the leper, the tax collector, the prostitute, and the outcast. His ministry was not one of selective fellowship but radical inclusion. He shared meals with sinners before they repented. He defended the woman caught in adultery before she changed her ways. His embrace was not contingent on performance—it was the beginning of transformation.

When the Church reflects this same spirit, it stops being a gatekeeper and becomes a greeter. It does not sort people by perceived worthiness. It simply says, "Come. There is room."

To emulate Jesus' hospitality means creating environments where everyone has access to grace, not just the insiders, not just the doctrinally aligned, not just the socially acceptable. It means loving people first, listening long, and letting the Holy Spirit do the work of conviction and change.

We must resist the urge to merely mirror the culture around us. The world does not need a church that simply reflects its own image—it longs for a community that is different, not because it is self-righteous, but because it radiates hope, truth, and healing. That is not always comfortable. In fact, it often confronts us with our own limitations and challenges us to grow. But that very discomfort can become sacred ground where transformation begins.

This is more than posture—it is practice. Churches must rethink the structure of their small groups, their entry points for service, and the tone of their messages. Welcoming is not just about having greeters at the door—it is about cultivating a whole culture of embrace.

Avoiding the Gatekeeper Mentality

The gatekeeper mentality manifests in subtle ways: the guarded glances, the insider language, and the unspoken rules about who is allowed to serve or belong. It shows up when someone walks through our doors and does not look the part, and we instinctively judge.

Gatekeeping is about control. It is about protecting a version of the church that feels safe, familiar, and unchallenged. However, the gospel is disruptive. Jesus was constantly disrupting the comfort of the religious elite to make space for the excluded.

We must ask hard questions:
- Do our churches reflect the diversity of our communities?
- Are we building spaces where newcomers are welcomed as guests, not evaluated as threats?
- Do we celebrate people who come to faith from messy backgrounds, or silently wish they would clean up faster?

We must also evaluate the culture of our leadership. Have we surrounded ourselves with "safe" voices who reflect our preferences, or have we made room for people with different stories, struggles, and perspectives? Inclusion does not dilute the gospel—it demonstrates it.

Making the Church the Safest Place to Fall

Every person who enters a church carries invisible burdens—wounds, regrets, fears. The Church should be the one place where they can set those burdens down without fear of rejection.

Too often, it is not safe. Too often, confession is met with consequences, not compassion. Doubt is met with discipline, not dialogue. Struggle is met with shame, not support.

What if the Church became the safest place to fall?

What if, like the father in the parable of the prodigal son, we ran to meet the broken before they had rehearsed their apology? What if our posture was not, "How did you get here?" but "I am so glad you came."

A gospel of welcome is not soft on sin—it is strong on grace. It trusts that when people are truly seen and loved, they are more likely to change than when they are shamed and excluded. It places hospitality at the center of our theology, not the edges.

A practical gospel of welcome also changes our language. We stop asking, "What is wrong with them?" and start asking, "What has wounded them?" We stop leading with expectations and begin with empathy. We train our greeters to notice the one who looks lost. We shape our preaching with sensitivity to those still hurting. We invite mess into the pews and believe that God will meet people there.

This is what Jesus did. This is what He still does. Moreover, this is what His Church must rediscover: a gospel that opens doors, not guards gates—a gospel that truly makes the church the safest place to fall.

When we do, something beautiful happens.

A welcoming church does not lower the bar of holiness—it opens the door to healing. It does not compromise truth—it embodies it with compassion. When grace is no longer gated, when the broken are not treated as burdens, and when love outpaces judgment, the Church becomes what it was always meant to be: a home for the hurting, a refuge for the restless, and a community where prodigals, doubters, and saints can sit at the same table. This is the gospel of welcome—and it is good news for us all.

29
Signs of a Restored Church

> "By this everyone will know that you
> are my disciples, if you love one another."
> — John 13:35

Measuring Health by Grace, Not Growth

For generations, the metrics of a "successful" church have too often mirrored the marketplace: bigger buildings, larger attendance, expanded budgets. However, a restored church does not measure health by the number of people in pews or the polish of its programs—it measures it by grace.

Is grace the atmosphere people breathe when they walk through the door? Is there room to struggle, to ask questions, to grow at the pace of real life and not just the church calendar?

A grace-filled church makes space for stories. It resists the temptation to commodify spirituality. It knows that Jesus left the ninety-nine for the one, and so it celebrates not just crowd size but individual restoration.

The Presence of the Spirit in Restored Relationships

When the Spirit of God is at work in a community, it shows up most clearly in the way people treat each other. Paul's list of the fruit of the Spirit (Galatians 5:22–23) is not abstract theology—it is a blueprint for Spirit-filled community: love, joy, peace, patience, kindness, goodness, faithfulness, gentleness, self-control.

Community is not just lived out on Sunday morning, but starts to fill the week. Love and concern become the hallmark of relationships. This means calls during the week just to check in. It looks like impromptu meals shared on a Tuesday, rides to doctor's appointments, and helping with moving furniture. It looks like showing up in each other's lives beyond the bulletin and the building.

These fruits are not produced by strategy but by surrender. They appear when leaders stop managing their image and start walking in humility, when congregants forgive freely, and when people stop pretending and start participating.

Restored churches are marked by restored relationships. Former enemies worship together. Long-held grudges are released. People speak the truth in love, and actually stay. There is laughter. There are tears. There is presence.

Healing Communities in a Fractured World

The church is not just a place for healing—it is a place of healing. A restored church does not hoard hope for itself. It becomes a refuge for the broken and a signpost of possibility in a weary world.

This healing posture is evident in how the church responds to injustice, welcomes the marginalized, and listens to the wounded. It is in the invitation extended to the single parent, the person with a substance abuse disorder, the skeptic, and the burned-out believer. It is in a church that looks more like a family than a club.

Signs of a Restored Church

Traits of a Spirit-Formed Community

A restored church does not guess at what it means to be healthy—it returns to the biblical blueprint. Here are several traits drawn from Scripture, reframed in everyday language, along with what they look like in practice:

A Culture of Care — Jesus said love is our greatest witness (John 13:34–35). In a healthy church, care is not relegated to a ministry team; it is everyone's instinct. Newcomers feel it. Long-timers share it. Hospitality is the culture, not the committee.

Rooted and Real — The early church was grounded in truth and anchored in community (Acts 2:42). This means Scripture is not cherry-picked to fit opinions, and small groups are not just social, they are spiritual support systems.

Carrying Each Other's Weight — Paul called us to bear one another's burdens (Galatians 6:2). That looks like casseroles and childcare, rides to chemo, and quiet presence in grief. It is the slow, faithful work of showing up.

Unity Without Uniformity — The church is one body with many parts (1 Corinthians 12). In a restored church, difference does not divide—it enriches. People worship side-by-side across political, racial, and generational lines, and find joy in what they share rather than fear in what they do not.

Open-Handed Living — Generosity in Acts was not manipulated—it was voluntary and joyful (Acts 4:32–35). Healthy churches give with gladness, sharing not only money, but space, skill, and time. Needs are noticed—and met—quietly and quickly.

Peacemaking as a Practice — Jesus blessed the peacemakers (Matthew 5:9). Peacemaking is not avoiding conflict—it is leaning into it with humility and hope. It means choosing resolution over resentment and keeping the table open.

Prayer as Lifeblood — Prayer was not a warm-up—it was the work (Acts 1:14). In Spirit-formed communities, prayer leaks into everything—planning, listening, grieving, dreaming. It is not just scheduled; it is spontaneous and shared.

Grace-Filled Accountability — Correction is not condemnation. Discipline is done relationally and redemptively (Matthew 18:15–17). Conversations happen in love, not legalism. People are not punished into change; they are invited into healing.

Healing from the Inside Out — A healthy church acknowledges collective wounds. It does not rush past its past. It seeks healing through honesty, through lament, and through listening to those it once ignored. It learns from failure instead of covering it up.

Truth with Tenderness — Speaking the truth in love (Ephesians 4:15) is an act of maturity. In restored churches, hard conversations are had with tenderness and care. Leaders do not weaponize Scripture; they embody it.

Everyone Has a Voice — A Spirit-filled church is not a spectator event—it is a participation movement (1 Corinthians 14:26). People bring their gifts, not just their attendance. Testimonies are shared. Questions are welcomed. Everyone matters.

Joy That Defies the Headlines — Restored churches are not immune to sorrow, but they are anchored in a joy that goes deeper than mood. It is the joy of the gospel. It is the strength to sing even in the dark. This joy is not loud, but lasting.

Love That Lives Beyond Sunday — Real community does not end with the benediction. In restored churches, Monday through Saturday is filled with connection. People text each other encouragement. Meals are shared. Hospital visits happen. Help is offered without being asked. The church becomes a village of care.

Outreach that Feels Like Welcome — Outreach in a restored church is not an event—it is a lifestyle. It is not a bait-and-switch program—it is presence. The neighborhood knows the church by its compassion, not just its convictions. Members mentor at schools, support local food pantries, walk with the lonely, and advocate for justice. It is consistent, faithful, and humble.

These are not just ideals. They are evidence. They are not signs of a perfect church, but of a church that has been touched by grace and is committed to growing.

A restored church will not be perfect. It will not always be popular, but it will be holy ground.

It will feel more like a family than a factory. More like a community than a campaign. It will preach Christ crucified—and risen—in both word and practice.

In a world fractured by image, ideology, and isolation, a restored church becomes a radical act of hope. It dares to be honest. It chooses humility. It opens wide the doors. In doing so, it becomes not only a sign of what God can do, but of what He is already doing.

This is the Church the world needs. This is the Church Jesus died for, and the one He is restoring.

30
Becoming the Church Jesus Died For

> *"I will build my church, and the gates of hell shall not prevail against it."* — Matthew 16:18

A Vision for the Future

What if the Church truly looked like Jesus?

What if it was known more for its mercy than its marketing? For its humility, not its hierarchy? For its healing presence, not its political power? What if it was marked by the patience to wait on God rather than by an obsession with sticking to a service schedule? What if we measured faithfulness not by how efficiently we moved through a Sunday agenda, but by how attentively we responded to the Spirit in our midst?

The Church Jesus died for is not a brand or a building; it is a community of believers. It is a people. A living body. A movement of grace and truth, forged in love and sent in power. It is not perfect, but it is repentant. It is not without scars, but honest about them. It does not pretend to be the answer to every question, but it refuses to run from the hard ones.

We are not called to maintain appearances. We are called to be ambassadors of a kingdom that turns everything upside down: where the last are first, where the poor are blessed, where the meek inherit the earth. This is not the church of celebrity, self-protection, or institutional fear. This is the Church that lives like Jesus, walks like Jesus, and welcomes like Jesus.

This is the Church the world is aching for.

The Church as a Place of Hope and Healing

Imagine a sanctuary where confession is not a rare occurrence, but rather a regular practice. Where testimonies do not just come from the triumphant, but from the broken-in-process. Where altar calls are not a production, but a pause for mercy. Imagine worship that dares to leave space for silence, lament, and the gritty work of waiting on God.

Imagine a church where grace is not a doctrine—it is the atmosphere. A place where people are not measured by how put-together they look, but by how honestly they walk. Where someone can walk in carrying addiction, grief, doubt, or shame, and still find belonging.

Where no one is too messy, too far gone, or too complicated to be embraced. This Church does not exist to guard the gate, but to hold open the door.

It speaks the truth, yes—but it does so tenderly. It names sin, but not as a weapon. It names sin as the thing Jesus came to free us from. It does not mock the lost. It searches for them. It does not shame the fallen. It bends to restore them. Hope flows when healing is not just a sermon topic but a lived experience, when we trade polished performances for honest presence, when the pews are filled not just with the well-dressed but with the worn-down, when the church dares to be less of a stage and more of a sanctuary.

Furthermore, this hope spills beyond the walls. A church that heals on the inside becomes a church that serves on the outside. It shows up in prisons, shelters, schools, and street corners. It welcomes refugees, embraces addicts, feeds the hungry, and advocates for the voiceless. It does not just preach reconciliation—it practices it, in homes and neighborhoods and public squares. It restores marriages, renews broken communities, and radiates the love of Christ into dark places.

This is not weakness. This is witness. The world sees Jesus not through our perfection, but through our repentance. Through our grace. Through our love.

Benediction: The Unrepentant Church Repents

We have looked in the mirror and seen our stains. We have covered up what God called us to confess. We have favored image over integrity. We have run programs instead of running after people. We have disciplined without discipling. We have spoken of holiness, yet we have avoided humility.

Nevertheless, the story is not over.

The Church can still repent. And it must. Not just with statements, but with systems. Not just with apologies, but with accountability. Not just with tears, but with truth.

To repent is not to dwell in shame. It is to return to the heart of the gospel: a Savior who runs to meet us, robes us in mercy, and calls us His own.

The unrepentant Church can still become the radiant bride Christ longs to return for— again.

So let us become that Church.

Let us lead with love.

Let us worship in spirit and truth. Let us correct with grace.

Let us walk with the wounded. Let us stand for the outcast.

Let us die to image and rise in integrity.

Let us not build monuments to ourselves, but movements of mercy. Let us repent.

Moreover, let us rise.

A Prayer of Repentance

Lord Jesus,
We come not with pretense, but with poverty of spirit. We lay down our pride, our programs, and our posturing. We confess that we have made idols of image and reputation, that we have chased crowds but not always carried the cross.
Forgive us.
Forgive us for the times we traded compassion for control, for when we silenced confession and elevated performance. Forgive us for guarding our gates more fiercely than we opened our arms. For every wounded soul that found judgment instead of mercy at our hands,
Lord, have mercy.
We repent of the sins we justified and the truths we hid. We repent of apathy, of cynicism, of spiritual arrogance. We repent of believing we could build your Church without your presence.
Restore to us the joy of our salvation. Break our hearts for what breaks Yours. Give us tears for the lost, and grace for the fallen. Teach us to walk humbly, love deeply, and live truthfully.
May we become a people who welcome the prodigal, bind up the broken, and dare to believe that redemption is always possible.
We are not finished. You are still shaping us.
May the Church rise again—not in its own strength, but in the beauty of repentance, clothed in mercy, radiant with hope.
Amen..

Study Guide

Introduction

This 13-week study guide is designed to walk your group through *The Unrepentant Church* in a way that is deeply personal, spiritually communal, and practically transformational. Whether used from the pulpit, in Sunday school, or around a living room, it provides a structure for meaningful reflection and honest growth.

While the format is built around a calendar, the heart of this journey cannot be confined to weeks alone. The real goal is not completion, but conversion. Not the kind that changes your label, but the kind that changes your heart, your church, and your relationships.

Each week includes:
- A time of confession
- Key Scripture readings
- Reflection and discussion questions
- Testimony prompts
- Action steps for personal and communal practice

It is recommended that each person in a group has a journal to record their own thoughts and reflections as they consider this material.

You'll also find optional symbolic actions—like communion, foot washing, or anointing—that can help embody the message in sacred, memorable ways.

This guide assumes that healing is messy, restoration takes courage, and that grace is the only climate where lasting transformation can grow. May it be a tool in your hands and a spark in your spirit.

Optional Communion Prompt

If your church practices communion, consider incorporating it during these sessions, especially on weeks that focus on repentance, restoration, or grace (e.g., Weeks 4, 6, and 12). Communion can become a sacred act of shared confession, healing, and remembrance.

Suggested moments:
- After the Time of Confession
- Following a testimony
- As a final act of worship

Invite participants to reflect on Christ's broken body and shed blood as the foundation of all restoration. Communion becomes the table where we're reminded: we all come empty-handed and all are welcome.

Optional Foot Washing Prompt

Consider incorporating a symbolic act of foot washing during Week 6 or Week 10—weeks that emphasize grace-filled discipleship and servant-hearted leadership.

Foot washing can:
- Embody humility and mutual care
- Break down status or role barriers within the group
- Prepare hearts for confession, restoration, or communion

Suggested moments:
- After testimony sharing
- Following the Time of Confession
- As a closing gesture of spiritual equality and grace

Participants may wash each other's hands as a modest alternative if foot washing is impractical.

Optional Script for Foot Washing:

"On the night He was betrayed, Jesus rose from the table, took a towel, and washed His disciples' feet. He said, 'Now that

I, your Lord and Teacher, have washed your feet, you also should wash one another's feet.' (John 13:14)

As you take part in this act today, let it be a sign of your willingness to serve, forgive, and walk humbly with each other."

Optional Anointing Prompt

Consider incorporating a symbolic act of anointing during Week 10 (A Restoring Church) or Week 13 (Worship That Tells the Truth). This sacred act embodies unity, calling, and the covering grace of God.

Scripture:

"How good and pleasant it is when God's people live together in unity... It is like precious oil poured on the head, running down on the beard..." —Psalm 133:1–2

Symbolic Insight:

Anointing oil in Scripture was deeply fragrant and long-lasting. For Aaron and the priests, it covered the scent of sacrifice-the smelly, messy, and bloody work of ministry—with something holy and beautiful. In the same way, grace does not erase our wounds; it covers them with the fragrance of Christ.

Suggested Use:
- Lightly anoint foreheads or hands with fragrant oil (e.g., frankincense or myrrh blend).
- May follow a time of testimony, confession, or restoration.
- Use in pairs or from a group leader.

Optional Script for Anointing:

"We anoint you not because you're perfect, but because you're called. As Aaron bore the scent of sacrifice, may you carry the fragrance of grace. May this oil remind you that your scars are not shame—they are your ministry."

Week 1:
Recognizing the Wound

Ch. 1: A Church That Lost Its Way
Ch. 2: Grace as the Defining Mark of Christ

Focus:
How the Church shifted from a grace-centered mission to image control. What does real grace look like?

Opening Scripture Reading

Begin by reading aloud: **Luke 15:1–7** – *The lost sheep and the joy of recovery.* Let it set the tone for the session.

Time of Confession

Invite participants to silently confess areas where they've contributed to image-based religion, withheld grace, or prioritized appearance over transformation.

Prayer prompt: "Lord, show us where we've lost sight of Your heart. Help us exchange performance for presence, and shame for grace."

Reflection Questions (Personal Notes)

1. Where have I experienced the difference between performance-based and grace-based church culture?
2. Have I ever felt like I had to hide my brokenness in church? What did that do to my spiritual life?
3. What does grace mean to me, truly, practically, right now?

Discussion Questions (Group Conversation)

1. What do we mean when we say the Church "lost its way"?
2. How can we distinguish between healthy holiness and harmful image management?

3. What would change if grace, not image, became our guiding principle?

Testimony Prompt

Invite someone to share a story of when they experienced rejection or unexpected grace from the Church.

Scriptures for Meditation

- Luke 15:1–7 – *The lost sheep and the joy of recovery*
- John 1:14 – *Jesus came full of grace and truth*
- Galatians 1:6–7 – *A warning against turning to "another gospel"*
- Isaiah 29:13 – *"They honor me with their lips, but their hearts are far from me"*

Action Points

- Spend 15 minutes this week journaling a personal story of grace or rejection in church.
- Ask God to show you one person to extend grace to this week—in word or action.
- As a group, brainstorm one practical way your church could better embody grace.
- Set aside 5–10 minutes of silence each day to ask, "Lord, where have I lost grace?" Allow space for conviction without shame.

Closing Blessing

"May the God of all grace, who called you to His eternal glory in Christ, restore, confirm, strengthen, and establish you." —1 Peter 5:10

Week 2:
The Culture of Rejection

Ch. 3: A Culture That Devours Its Wounded
Ch. 4: Rejection in the Name of Holiness

Focus:

When churches punish the broken instead of restoring them. What is the cost of spiritual cleanliness without compassion?

Opening Scripture Reading

Begin by reading aloud: **Matthew 9:10–13** – *"I desire mercy, not sacrifice."*

Time of Confession

Invite participants to consider moments when they've rejected others in the name of rules, or withheld grace in fear of seeming soft on sin.

Prayer prompt: "God of mercy, forgive us for the times we prioritized purity over people, and fear over love."

Reflection Questions (Personal Notes)

1. Have I ever felt rejected by the church because of failure, struggle, or sin?
2. Have I ever participated actively or passively in the rejection of others?
3. What would it look like to extend mercy instead of judgment?

Discussion Questions (Group Conversation)

1. What motivates churches to devour their wounded: fear, tradition, or something else?
2. Can holiness and mercy coexist in church discipline?

3. What changes when we see rejection not as a safeguard but as a wound?

Testimony Prompt

Invite someone to share a story about being welcomed after failure, or about healing from church rejection.

Scriptures for Meditation

- Matthew 9:10–13 – *"It is not the healthy who need a doctor, but the sick."*
- Hosea 6:6 – *"I desire mercy, not sacrifice."*
- Romans 2:4 – *God's kindness leads us to repentance*
- Luke 18:9–14 – *The parable of the Pharisee and the tax collector*

Action Points

- Write a note or message of encouragement to someone whom the Church has hurt.
- Reflect on areas where your church culture may equate holiness with exclusion.
- Commit to one merciful action this week—respond to failure with kindness.
- Look for someone who may feel like an outsider—greet them, include them, listen without fixing.

Closing Blessing

"The Lord is compassionate and gracious, slow to anger, abounding in love." —Psalm 103:8

Week 3: Washing Your Hands, or Their Feet

Ch. 5: When the Wounded Are Blamed

Ch. 6: Grace for the Guilty

Focus:
How shame and blame keep people from healing. How can grace meet guilt head-on?

Opening Scripture Reading

Begin by reading aloud: **John 8:1–11** – *The woman caught in adultery: "Let the one without sin cast the first stone."*

Time of Confession

Invite participants to reflect on moments they have blamed others to protect themselves, or when they withheld grace because guilt made them uncomfortable.

Prayer prompt: "Lord, help us trade accusation for empathy. Show us how to reflect Your grace to those who feel unworthy."

Reflection Questions (Personal Notes)

1. Have I ever used blame to avoid dealing with someone's pain—or my own?
2. Do I find it easier to blame or to forgive? Why?
3. How does guilt change when it is met with grace?

Discussion Questions (Group Conversation)

1. In what ways does the image of Pilate washing his hands (Matt. 27:24) contrast with Jesus washing His disciples' feet (John 13:5)?
2. How does blame function as a way of "washing our hands" of responsibility in church culture?

3. What would it look like for our church to move from distancing blame to drawing near in service?

Testimony Prompt

Invite someone to share how grace changed the outcome of a failure in their life, or how blame delayed healing.

Scriptures for Meditation

- John 8:1–11 – *The woman caught in adultery*
- Psalm 32:1–5 – *Blessed is the one whose sins are forgiven*
- James 5:16 – *Confess your sins to one another and pray for each other so that you may be healed*
- Romans 8:1 – *There is no condemnation for those in Christ Jesus*

Action Points

- Reflect on someone you have quietly blamed—pray for them this week.
- Write a note of grace to someone carrying guilt.
- As a group, commit to interrupting blame language when you hear it in conversation or leadership.
- At least once this week, respond to a mistake—yours or someone else's—with unexpected gentleness.

Closing Blessing

"Therefore encourage one another and build one another up, just as you are doing." —1 Thessalonians 5:11

Week 4:
Replacing Rejection with Redemption

Ch. 7: Rejection, Not Redemption
Ch. 8: When the Church Repents

Focus:
Repentance is the doorway to renewal. How can churches model confession and turn from performative religion?

Opening Scripture Reading

Begin by reading aloud: **2 Corinthians 7:9–10** – *"Godly sorrow brings repentance that leads to salvation and leaves no regret."*

Time of Confession

Invite participants to consider places where they've favored judgment over redemption or resisted corporate repentance because of pride or fear.

Prayer prompt: "Lord, forgive us for choosing rejection over restoration. Teach us to repent boldly and lead redemptively."

Reflection Questions (Personal Notes)

1. How have I seen the Church use rejection as a substitute for dealing with sin?
2. What keeps me (or us) from repenting—fear, shame, pride, reputation?
3. What would it look like for me personally to model a redemptive response?

Discussion Questions (Group Conversation)

1. Why do churches sometimes prefer removing people over restoring them?
2. What does true repentance look like on a church-wide level?

3. How does modeling redemption publicly affect those outside the church?

Testimony Prompt

Invite someone to share how repentance—personal or communal—opened the door to healing and redemption in their life.

Scriptures for Meditation

- 2 Corinthians 7:9–10 – *Godly sorrow leads to repentance*
- Luke 19:1–10 – *Zacchaeus: repentance and restitution*
- Joel 2:12–13 – *"Return to me with all your heart"*
- Revelation 3:19 – *"Those whom I love I rebuke and discipline. So be earnest and repent."*

Action Points

- Reflect on an area where you need to repent, not just feel bad. Make a move toward restoration.
- As a group, discuss one area where your church or small group could model corporate repentance.
- Reach out to someone who has felt rejected by the church—apologize or listen if needed.
- Choose one redemptive action this week that repairs a relationship or heals a wound.

Closing Blessing

"Return to the Lord your God, for he is gracious and compassionate, slow to anger and abounding in love." —Joel 2:13

Week 5:
Becoming a Grace Culture

Ch. 9: The Culture of Grace
Ch. 10: From Control to Compassion

Focus:

Replacing fear-driven systems with compassion. What does a grace-first church look like?

Opening Scripture Reading

Begin by reading aloud: **Micah 6:8** – *"What does the Lord require of you? To act justly, love mercy, and walk humbly with your God."*

Time of Confession

Invite participants to reflect on moments when they contributed to a culture of fear or performance—whether in leadership, conversation, or silent expectation.

Prayer prompt: "Jesus, let our culture mirror Yours—one that sees, forgives, and restores. Replace our fear with Your compassion."

Reflection Questions (Personal Notes)

1. Have I ever used control or shame to enforce change in someone or myself?
2. How has compassion helped me grow more than correction ever did?
3. What kind of atmosphere do I personally help create at church?

Discussion Questions (Group Conversation)

1. What are signs of a fear-driven system in a church?
2. How do we balance boundaries with grace in leadership?

Study Guide

3. What would it look like for compassion, not image or policy, to be our first impulse?

Testimony Prompt

Invite someone to share a story of how compassion in church changed their spiritual growth or restored their faith.

Scriptures for Meditation

- Micah 6:8 – *Act justly, love mercy, walk humbly*
- Matthew 23:4 – *"They tie up heavy loads… but aren't willing to lift a finger"*
- Romans 12:10 – *Be devoted to one another in love*
- 1 Peter 4:8 – *Love covers a multitude of sins*

Action Points

- Identify one way you've been operating out of control—ask God for help releasing it.
- Offer someone a compassionate response when they expect judgment.
- As a group, brainstorm structural or leadership changes that promote a grace-first environment.
- Speak one encouraging word this week to someone who is spiritually struggling. Let grace lead your tongue.

Closing Blessing

"The Lord is gracious and righteous; our God is full of compassion."
—Psalm 116:5

Week 6:
Discipleship Done Right

Ch. 11: Discipleship That Heals
Ch. 12: The Ministry of Restoration

Focus:

Discipleship must reflect grace, not image management. How can restoration become part of our discipleship culture?

Opening Scripture Reading

Begin by reading aloud: **1 Thessalonians 2:7–8** – *"We were gentle among you... because you had become so dear to us."*

Time of Confession

Invite participants to reflect on where they have made discipleship about conformity instead of compassion.

Prayer prompt: "Jesus, forgive us for creating followers of ourselves instead of You. Teach us to disciple with grace, patience, and love."

Reflection Questions (Personal Notes)

1. Has my idea of discipleship been more about control or care?
2. What has healed me more: correction or connection?
3. How could restoration become a core part of how I disciple others?

Discussion Questions (Group Conversation)

1. What unhealthy models of discipleship have we seen in churches?
2. How can we shift from performance-based mentoring to healing-based mentoring?
3. What are the dangers of discipleship without grace?

Testimony Prompt

Invite someone to share how a mentor helped restore them spiritually—or how rigid discipleship wounded them.

Scriptures for Meditation

- 1 Thessalonians 2:7–8 – *Gentle like a nursing mother*
- John 21:15–19 – *Jesus restores Peter and commissions him*
- 2 Timothy 2:24–25 – *The Lord's servant must be kind to everyone*
- Proverbs 27:6 – *Wounds from a friend can be trusted*

Action Points

- Identify one person you are influencing—pray about how to become a safe space for them.
- Reflect on your own discipleship experiences—what would you replicate, and what would you redeem?
- As a group, discuss how to build a culture where discipleship includes failure, grace, and restoration.
- Listen well this week. Let someone share their struggle without correcting them.

Closing Blessing

"He who began a good work in you will carry it on to completion until the day of Christ Jesus." —Philippians 1:6

Week 7:
The Path of Restoration (Part 1)

Ch. 13: Step 1: When Truth Breaks the Silence
Ch. 14: Step 2: Care Before Control
Ch. 15: Step 3: Listening for the Wound

Focus:

The beginning of healing includes truth, care, and attentive listening.

Opening Scripture Reading

Begin by reading aloud: **James 5:16** – *"Confess your sins to one another and pray for each other so that you may be healed."*

Time of Confession

Invite participants to reflect on times they have ignored, silenced, or rushed past someone's pain rather than listening to it.

Prayer prompt: "Lord, give us the courage to speak truth and the compassion to hear it. Help us lead with care, not control."

Reflection Questions (Personal Notes)

1. Why is truth-telling such a powerful first step in restoration?
2. Have I been tempted to offer solutions before offering care?
3. What does it mean to truly *listen for the wound* in someone else?

Discussion Questions (Group Conversation)

1. What keeps churches from creating space for honest confession and truth-telling?

2. How does "care before control" challenge the way we typically handle sin?
3. Why is listening such a critical part of healing?

Testimony Prompt

Invite someone to share a time when they felt heard and supported after telling a hard truth, or when someone's care changed the direction of their healing.

Scriptures for Meditation

- James 5:16 – *Confess and pray for one another*
- Proverbs 20:5 – *The purposes of a person's heart are deep waters, but one who has insight draws them out*
- Matthew 18:15 – *Go to your brother when they sin*
- Galatians 6:1–2 – *Restore gently… carry one another's burdens*

Action Points

- Identify one relationship where truth has been avoided—pray for courage and grace to open a conversation.
- Practice *care before control* this week in a moment of conflict—focus on compassion, not fixing.
- As a group, discuss how your church can become a safer space for people to speak the truth.
- This week, spend intentional time just listening to someone's story without evaluating it.

Closing Blessing

"Let your conversation be always full of grace, seasoned with salt." — Colossians 4:6

Week 8:
The Path of Restoration (Part 2)

Ch. 16: Step 4: Healing from the Inside Out
Ch. 17: Step 5: Accountability That Restores
Ch. 18: Step 6: Restoration with Wisdom

Focus:
Graceful, structured accountability leads to transformation, not image repair.

Opening Scripture Reading
Begin by reading aloud: **Galatians 6:1–2** – *"Restore gently… carry one another's burdens."*

Time of Confession
Invite participants to reflect on times they have sought quick fixes, withheld accountability out of fear, or used it as punishment rather than support.

Prayer prompt: "Father, help us walk with others through slow, honest healing. Teach us to carry, not crush."

Reflection Questions (Personal Notes)
1. When have I experienced deep, lasting healing rather than a surface fix?
2. How does healthy accountability feel different than control or shame?
3. What kind of wisdom do I need to offer grace and truth together?

Discussion Questions (Group Conversation)
1. What distinguishes redemptive accountability from punitive correction?

Study Guide

2. How can we support someone's healing without overstepping or rescuing?
3. Why is wisdom essential to walking through restoration with others?

Testimony Prompt

Invite someone to share how wise, grace-filled accountability shaped their healing journey—or how its absence caused harm.

Scriptures for Meditation

- Galatians 6:1–2 – *Restore gently, carry burdens*
- Proverbs 4:7 – *"Wisdom is supreme—get wisdom."*
- Hebrews 12:11 – *Discipline yields a harvest of righteousness*
- 2 Corinthians 1:3–4 – *God comforts us so we can comfort others*

Action Points

- Reach out to someone you trust and ask for one area of accountability you can grow in.
- Reflect on a time you tried to "fix" someone—how would you handle it differently now?
- As a group, develop simple "restoration guidelines" that protect dignity and promote healing.
- Offer someone grace and truth this week—a hard word wrapped in love and presence.

Closing Blessing

"The wisdom that comes from heaven is first of all pure; then peace-loving, considerate, submissive, full of mercy and good fruit." —James 3:17

Week 9:
The Ripple Effects

Ch. 19: Collateral Damage and Secondary Wounds
Ch. 20: When the Fallen Refuse Help

Focus:

How do we care for those affected by moral failure, including when the offender will not receive restoration?

Opening Scripture Reading

Begin by reading aloud: **Romans 12:15** – *"Rejoice with those who rejoice; mourn with those who mourn."*

Time of Confession

Invite participants to reflect on how they have responded to those caught in the crossfire of church conflict or failure—have they been overlooked, silenced, or blamed?

Prayer prompt: "Lord, give us compassion for the silent sufferers. Teach us to see the wounded behind the headlines and bring comfort to those left in the rubble."

Reflection Questions (Personal Notes)

1. Have I been affected by someone else's fall? How did I process it?
2. Have I unintentionally added to someone's pain by staying silent or looking away?
3. What does it look like to help someone grieve spiritual betrayal or loss?

Discussion Questions (Group Conversation)

1. Why do secondary wounds often go unaddressed in churches?
2. How can we support people when the person at fault refuses help or restoration?

Study Guide

3. What kind of healing structure could care for the wounded on the periphery?

Testimony Prompt

Invite someone to share how a leader's fall affected their spiritual journey—and what helped (or hindered) their healing afterward.

Scriptures for Meditation

- Romans 12:15 – *Mourn with those who mourn*
- Ezekiel 34:4 – *"You have not strengthened the weak or bound up the injured…"*
- 2 Corinthians 1:3–4 – *The God of all comfort*
- Matthew 5:4 – *"Blessed are those who mourn, for they will be comforted."*

Action Points

- Reach out to someone you know who was impacted by a church wound—listen, honor, and support them.
- As a group, identify secondary wounds in your community and brainstorm ways to bring healing.
- Pray for those who still carry unspoken grief from spiritual loss.
- Offer space for lament—invite someone to tell their story without correcting or fixing it.

Closing Blessing

"The Lord is close to the brokenhearted and saves those who are crushed in spirit." —Psalm 34:18

Week 10:
A Restoring Church

Ch. 21: The Church as a Restoring Community
Ch. 22: Pastoring with Scars

Focus:

Restoration is central to the mission of the Church and its leaders. What does leadership look like when it comes from humility?

Opening Scripture Reading

Begin by reading aloud: **Isaiah 61:1–3** – *"He has sent me to bind up the brokenhearted… to bestow a crown of beauty instead of ashes."*

Time of Confession

Invite participants to consider where they have expected perfection from leaders, or feared leading because of their own scars.

Prayer prompt: "Lord, thank You for restoring the broken. Teach us to lead with humility, and to follow with grace."

Reflection Questions (Personal Notes)

1. Have I believed the lie that leaders must be flawless?
2. How might scars actually equip someone for deeper ministry?
3. What would a church of restorers look like?

Discussion Questions (Group Conversation)

1. Why does the Church often hide or disqualify wounded leaders?
2. What are the risks and rewards of leading with scars?
3. How can we cultivate a church culture where restoration is expected and honored?

Testimony Prompt

Invite someone to share how a humble, scarred leader helped them heal—or how they found strength in their own weakness.

Scriptures for Meditation

- Isaiah 61:1–3 – *Beauty for ashes; restoration as calling*
- 2 Corinthians 12:9 – *"My grace is sufficient… my power is made perfect in weakness"*
- John 20:27 – *Jesus invites Thomas to touch His scars*
- Galatians 6:1 – *Restore gently, watch yourself*

Action Points

- Reflect on one area where you need healing in order to lead more honestly.
- Encourage a leader you know by affirming how their humility has shaped you.
- As a group, name the gifts that wounded leaders bring to ministry.
- Write down one scar God has redeemed in your life. Consider how it might become a source of hope for others.

Closing Blessing

"The Lord rebuilds Jerusalem; He gathers the exiles of Israel. He heals the brokenhearted and binds up their wounds." —Psalm 147:2–3

Week 11:
Structures That Heal

Ch. 23: Structures That Serve the Spirit
Ch. 24: The Role of the Congregation

Focus:

Healthy systems and engaged congregations are necessary to sustain grace-based transformation.

Opening Scripture Reading

Begin by reading aloud: **Acts 6:1–4** – *The early church organizes to meet spiritual and practical needs.*

Time of Confession

Invite participants to reflect on how they have benefited from or contributed to unhealthy church systems, whether by compliance, silence, or fear.

Prayer prompt: "Lord, forgive us for the times we have maintained systems that silence rather than restore. Give us the courage to change what no longer serves You."

Reflection Questions (Personal Notes)

1. Have I ever experienced a church structure that hindered grace?
2. What kind of systems help me grow in safety and truth?
3. Where do I need to speak up or step up in my congregation?

Discussion Questions (Group Conversation)

1. How can church systems unintentionally protect image over people?
2. What does it look like for policies and leadership to support healing, not just control?
3. What role does the congregation play in keeping a church healthy?

Testimony Prompt

Invite someone to share a time when a church structure or lay leader helped—or hindered their spiritual healing or growth.

Scriptures for Meditation

- Acts 6:1–4 – *Creating new systems for better care*
- Proverbs 11:14 – *With many advisors, there is victory*
- 1 Corinthians 12:12–27 – *Every part of the body matters*
- Romans 12:4–8 – *Use your gifts to serve one another*

Action Points

- Reflect on how your church's structure encourages or inhibits grace.
- Have a conversation with a leader about how systems could shift toward healing.
- As a group, explore what shared responsibility (not just pastoral) looks like in spiritual restoration.
- Affirm a lay leader or volunteer who quietly helps others heal. Let them know their role matters.

Closing Blessing

"Let everything be done decently and in order"—*but let that order be rooted in grace.* —1 Corinthians 14:40 (adapted)

Week 12:
Corporate Repentance and Revival

Ch. 25: When Churches Repent
Ch. 26: The Power of Lament

Focus:

Churches must confess collectively. What does lament have to do with healing and revival?

Opening Scripture Reading

Begin by reading aloud: **Joel 2:12–13** – *"Return to me with all your heart… for he is gracious and compassionate."*

Time of Confession

Invite participants to reflect on collective wrongs the church has tolerated—whether silence, legalism, exclusion, or image protection.

Prayer prompt: "God of mercy, forgive us for the sins we have shared. Teach us to weep together, repent together, and rise together."

Reflection Questions (Personal Notes)

1. Where has my church needed to repent corporately but avoided it?
2. How do I feel about lament as a spiritual discipline?
3. What collective healing could come from shared confession?

Discussion Questions (Group Conversation)

1. Why is corporate repentance so rare in modern church life?

Study Guide

2. How does lament help a church process its pain and brokenness?
3. What would it look like for our group or church to model collective repentance?

Testimony Prompt

Invite someone to share how a church or group-wide confession or lament brought healing or revival.

Scriptures for Meditation

- Joel 2:12–13 – *"Return to me with all your heart"*
- Nehemiah 1:6–7 – *Nehemiah confesses the sins of his people*
- Psalm 51 – *A prayer of repentance*
- Lamentations 3:22–24 – *Hope rises out of lament*

Action Points

- Write a communal confession with your group this week. Pray it aloud together.
- Spend 10 minutes in personal lament for the Church— its failures, wounds, and missed opportunities.
- Consider holding a simple prayer night or time of silence for corporate confession.
- Engage in a symbolic act of repentance (e.g., writing down and burning confessions, washing hands, lighting candles).

Closing Blessing

"If my people, who are called by my name, will humble themselves and pray… then I will hear from heaven and heal their land." —2 Chronicles 7:14

Week 13: Worship That Tells the Truth

Ch. 27: The Sound of Honest Worship
Ch. 28: The Church with Open Arms
Ch. 29: Signs of a Restored Church
Ch. 30: Becoming the Church Jesus Died For

Focus:

Honest worship and inclusive community reflect a Church that has been transformed by grace.

Opening Scripture Reading

Begin by reading aloud: **John 4:23–24** – *"True worshipers will worship the Father in the Spirit and in truth."*

Time of Confession

Invite participants to reflect on ways the Church (or they personally) have prioritized appearance over authenticity in worship or community life.

Prayer prompt: "God, forgive us for making worship a performance and community a club. Teach us to love truthfully, worship honestly, and welcome freely."

Reflection Questions (Personal Notes)

1. What does 'worship in spirit and truth' mean to me?
2. When have I experienced a truly open and grace-filled church community?
3. How can I contribute to creating that kind of space for others?

Discussion Questions (Group Conversation)

1. Why is honest worship difficult for many churches to cultivate?
2. What are the marks of a restored church community?
3. How can our group become a place where people meet Jesus, not judgment?

Testimony Prompt

Invite someone to share how honest worship or an open community impacted their healing, faith, or sense of belonging.

Scriptures for Meditation

- John 4:23–24 – *Worship in spirit and in truth*
- Luke 7:36–50 – *A sinful woman's worship and Jesus' grace*
- Romans 15:7 – *Accept one another just as Christ accepted you*
- Psalm 51:17 – *A broken and contrite heart God will not despise*

Action Points

- Examine your personal worship this week: is it honest or performative? Ask God to deepen its sincerity.
- Invite someone into your spiritual community who may feel unwelcome in other places.
- As a group, identify one way to visibly signal openness and grace to outsiders.
- End your group time this week with 5 minutes of honest, unscripted praise—each person offering a line or word of worship from the heart.

Closing Blessing

"Now to Him who is able to do immeasurably more than all we ask or imagine... to Him be glory in the church and in Christ Jesus throughout all generations." —Ephesians 3:20–21

Acknowledgments

I wish to express deep gratitude to the voices—both ancient and modern—whose words have rooted in my life and are echoed throughout this book. Their insights have sharpened my thinking, stirred my heart, and helped bring clarity to the message of grace and restoration that *The Unrepentant Church* seeks to embody.

To the anonymous author of the quote, "The greatest harm done to the wounded is not their fall, but our refusal to kneel beside them"—your words have comforted many and speak volumes in silence.

To OpenAI's ChatGPT, whose assistance in organizing, scanning, and formatting this material proved invaluable in shaping this work into its clearest form—thank you for being a tool that empowered clarity and creativity.

And to Jesus Christ, whose teachings, actions, and presence are quoted and referenced throughout—may His model of radical love and grace shape us anew.

Biography

C.S. Lewis. *The Screwtape Letters.* New York: HarperOne, 2001.

Holy Bible: New International Version. Grand Rapids: Zondervan, 2011.

Unless otherwise noted, all Scripture quotations are from the Holy Bible, New International Version®. Copyright © 1973, 1978, 1984, 2011 by Biblica, Inc.™ Used by permission. All rights reserved worldwide.

- Isaiah 53:3 (NIV).
- Jeremiah 6:14 (NIV).
- Luke 5:31–32 (NIV).
- Matthew 5:9, 5:23, 16:18, 18:15–17 (NIV).
- John 13:34–35 (NIV).
- Acts 1:14, 2:42–47, 4:32–35 (NIV).
- Romans 12:15 (NIV).
- 1 Corinthians 12:12, 12:26, 14:26 (NIV).
- 2 Corinthians 3:17, 5:18–19 (NIV).
- Galatians 5:22, 6:2 (NIV).
- Ephesians 1:22, 4:15 (NIV).
- 1 Peter 4:17 (NIV).
- Psalm 34:18, 126:5 (NIV).

The Message: The Bible in Contemporary Language. Eugene H. Peterson. Colorado Springs, CO: NavPress, 2002. *Used by permission. All rights reserved.*

- Isaiah 1:13–17 (The Message)

St. Augustine. *Quote attributed, source unverified*: "The Church is not a museum for saints, but a hospital for sinners."

Unknown. *"The greatest harm done to the wounded is not their fall, but our refusal to kneel beside them."* Attribution unverified.

African Proverb. *Origin unknown. Traditional oral wisdom attributed to various African cultures*